APRIL
1 9 9 1

30

POLICY
ANALYSES IN
INTERNATIONAL
ECONOMICS

Economic Policy Coordination: Requiem or Prologue?

Wendy Dobson

INSTITUTE FOR INTERNATIONAL ECONOMICS

ECONOMIC POLICY COORDINATION: REQUIEM OR PROLOGUE?

ECONOMIC POLICY COORDINATION: REQUIEM OR PROLOGUE?

Wendy Dobson

INSTITUTE FOR INTERNATIONAL ECONOMICS
WASHINGTON, DC
April 1991

Wendy Dobson, Visiting Fellow at the Institute, is Senior Fellow at the Faculty of Management at the University of Toronto. She served as Associate Deputy Minister of Finance in the Canadian government (1987-89) and as Canada's G-7 deputy (1987–89). She was president of the C.D. Howe Institute (1981-87), and is the author of numerous articles and monographs on international economic relations and Canadian issues in macroeconomics and trade policy.

INSTITUTE FOR INTERNATIONAL ECONOMICS
11 Dupont Circle, NW
Washington, DC 20036-1207
(202) 328-9000   Telex: 261271 IIE UR   FAX: (202) 328-5432

C. Fred Bergsten, *Director*
Linda Griffin Kean, *Director of Publications*

The Institute for International Economics was created by, and receives substantial support from, the German Marshall Fund of the United States.

Printed in the United States of America 93 92 91   3 2 1

Library of Congress Catalog-in-Publication Data

Dobson, Wendy
    Economic policy coordination: requiem or prologue? / Wendy Dobson.
      p. cm.—(Policy analyses in international economics: 30)
    Includes bibliographical references (p. 159).
    ISBN 0-88132-102-8: $11.95
    1. International economic relations. 2. Economic policy. 3. International cooperation. 4. International finance. I. Title. II. Series.
HF1359.D64 1991   91-11640
338.9—dc20   CIP

Contents

FIGURES

Preface

International monetary issues have been a continuing focus of the research program of the Institute. We have published extensively on trade imbalances, exchange rates, and the international monetary system. Some of our major contributions to analysis and policy in this area have emerged through studies such as *Deficits and the Dollar: The World Economy at Risk,* by Stephen N. Marris, and *The Exchange Rate System,* by John Williamson.

In particular, we have tried to blend analysis of international monetary economics with appraisals of institutional arrangements such as the Group of Seven (G-7) and the International Monetary Fund. In *Targets and Indicators: A Blueprint for the International Coordination of Economic Policy,* for example, John Williamson and Marcus H. Miller offered comprehensive proposals for stabilizing the world economy by integrating the "reference ranges" for currencies adopted by the G-7 at the Louvre in 1987 into a scheme designed to give content to the "indicators" launched at the Tokyo summit in 1986 to improve policy coordination. On the institutional side, Yoichi Funabashi provided the definitive study to date of the G-7 process in his *Managing the Dollar: From the Plaza to Louvre.*

This new volume by Wendy Dobson combines the analytic and institutional dimensions in a study of the G-7 since 1986. She appraises the results of cooperative policies as well as the process by which they were developed and suggests improvements for the future. As a professional economist and former director of a leading research institution in Canada, as well as Canada's Associate Deputy Finance Minister and "G-7 Deputy" between 1987 and 1989, Dobson brings an unusual combination of perspectives to the study. We hope and believe that the study's combination of the substance and process of international financial diplomacy will provide an important contribution to thinking and future policy.

The Institute for International Economics is a private nonprofit institution for the study and discussion of international economic policy. Its purpose is to analyze important issues in that area, and to develop and communicate practical new approaches for dealing with them. The Institute is completely nonpartisan.

The Institute was created by a generous commitment of funds from the German Marshall Fund of the United States in 1981 and now receives about 12 percent of its support from that source. In addition, major institutional grants are now being received from the Ford Foundation, the William and Flora Hewlett Foundation, the William M. Keck, Jr. Foundation, the Alfred P. Sloan Foundation, the C. V. Starr Foundation, and the United States–Japan Foundation. A number of other foundations and private corporations are contributing to the highly diversified financial resources of the Institute. About 15 percent of those resources in our latest fiscal year were provided by contributors outside the United States, including about 5 percent from Japan.

The Board of Directors bears overall responsibility for the Institute and gives general guidance and approval to its research program—including identification of topics that are likely to become important to international economic policymakers over the medium run (generally, one to three years), and which thus should be addressed by the Institute. The Director, working closely with the staff and outside Advisory Committee, is responsible for the development of particular projects and makes the final decision to publish an individual study.

The Institute hopes that its studies and other activities will contribute to building a stronger foundation for international economic policy around the world. We invite readers of these publications to let us know how they think we can best accomplish this objective.

C. FRED BERGSTEN
Director
March 1991

Foreword

International economic policy coordination has a long and intermittent history. The latest chapter in its history began with the formation in 1985 of the so-called Group of Five, in the context of the economic summits of the leaders of five major industrialized nations of the West. The G-5 and later the G-7 have functioned in an informal way, for the most part independent of the existing major multilateral economic institutions. Although this lack of structure has promoted a frankness in the G-7's deliberations that is highly valued among the participants, it has also contributed to an ad hoc cooperative framework in which true policy coordination rarely has been practiced.

My own involvement as a G-7 participant began with an economist's skepticism: if the purpose of economic policy coordination is to manage the unwanted spillovers of one country's policies onto another, could not those spillovers be minimized if national governments followed sensible economic policies in the first place? Some of this skepticism was replaced as it became more apparent how much governments' domestic policy objectives and analytical frameworks can differ, and how far policymakers have yet to travel before they think in terms of the international as well as the domestic consequences of their policy options.

This study was motivated by the desire to compare theory with practice. In theory there is a lot more that successful coordination can do besides the concerted intervention in foreign-exchange markets that has so fascinated the media in recent years. But true coordination—of policies—is slow and unexciting because, as is well known, the time lag between the emergence of a problem and policymakers' recognition of it, and between recognition and implementation of a remedy, is long compared to the pace of change in modern economies.

The 1985–89 period—the first five years of operation of the G-7 coordination process—is the focus of much of this study. Five years is not long enough to allow definitive conclusions about the actual economic impact of coordination, in the sense that one can identify changes that would not have occurred in the absence of the process. It is long enough, however, to draw lessons for the future, which is the purpose of this study, for the increasing integration of the global economy means that policy cooperation undoubtedly does have a future.

The study is analytical in a reflective sense; it is a former practitioner's assessment, using measures similar to those actually employed in the process. It is, unfortunately, cryptic in places because of the confidentiality expected of former participants.

Although the analysis and conclusions are my own, I am indebted to many people who participated in the preparation of this study. C. Fred Bergsten provided continuous encouragement and critical insight—indeed it is difficult to find an institutional issue that he has not, at some time in his remarkable career, already thought or written about. The Institute for International Economics brought together a study group whose input was very helpful; that group included William Cline, John Williamson, C. Randall Henning, and Thomas Bayard from the Institute; Jeffrey Frankel of the University of California, Berkeley, who is also a fellow Visiting Fellow at the Institute; as well as Warwick McKibbin, Peter Hooper, Doug Purvis, Bob Solomon, Jacques Polak, and Horst Schulman. I am particularly grateful to Bill White and his colleagues at the Bank of Canada, and to Jacob Frenkel and Paul Masson and some of their colleagues at the International Monetary Fund.

Ted Truman, Peter Kenen, Stephen Marris, Richard Cooper, John Williamson, and Emil van Lennep deserve special thanks for sharing their time and extensive experience through thorough review of the manuscript.

Former colleagues in each of the G-7 treasuries and central banks and at the Organization for Economic Cooperation and Development provided valuable insights for which I am grateful; timely assistance and advice was received from former colleagues Howard Brown, Doug Nevison, and Susan Kalinowski at the Department of Finance in Ottawa.

Finally, my thanks go to Michael Treadway, Linda Griffin Kean, and their staff for their fine and speedy editorial and production services, and to Peter Uimonen for patient research assistance of the highest quality.

1 Introduction

A historian studying the business sections of newspapers from the 1950s would find a stark contrast between the economic headlines of that era and those of recent years. The daily economic news of the 1950s—especially on the international front—was reasonably tranquil: interest rates and exchange rates varied little; inflation was low in the industrialized countries; news about international trade flows and financial balances, when it made the papers at all, was buried in the back pages. By the 1980s, however, headlines were dominated by concerns about high interest rates, fiscal deficits, volatile exchange rates, and sharp swings in economic relationships among countries.

Uncertainty and rapid change, captured in these daily headlines, shift the very ground under the feet of businesses whose survival depends on international trade. International business travelers in the early 1980s found European producers complaining about high real interest rates and economic stagnation, while American goods exporters, like the head of Caterpillar, Inc., were publicizing the uneven effects of the strong dollar on the US economy. Yet by 1986 Japanese exporters were observed to be deeply troubled by the potential loss of foreign market share due to a weakened dollar and a strong yen. The accelerated pace and profound impact of these changes have caused a shift in public awareness of the international economic environment that is dramatically captured outside the main railway station in downtown Tokyo. There passers-by need only glance up at a huge lighted sign to check the latest yen-dollar exchange rate.

Underlying this increasing economic turbulence have been fundamental changes in the structures of the world's goods and capital markets—the result of advances in communications technology and changes in the economic policies that provide the rules of the global game. Trade barriers have declined; controls have been removed from international capital markets; domestic financial institutions have been deregulated. The industrial economies are becoming ever more interdependent—more like one economy. Tighter economic links among countries have reduced the ability of policymakers to manage what is happening in their own country, as the effects of economic policies in one country are transmitted ever more readily to its trading and investment partners. Policy changes quickly spill over, through the impact of exchange and interest rate changes, to affect international asset flows, trade flows, current accounts, and inflation.

In contrast, political structures in most of the industrialized countries have changed little since World War II. With the notable exception of Western Europe, the world retains much of its traditional segmentation along the lines of nation-states. Yet national economic policymakers now face the challenge of adapting to the dramatic integration of markets. Traditionally autonomous in their decision making, they must now take into account the impact of spillovers from their policies. In the absence of global institutions to manage an increasingly integrated world economy, interdependence must be jointly managed by the nation-states themselves.

In the second half of the 1980s, joint management of global economic relationships has been attempted through an informal, loosely organized process of consultation and negotiation among the treasuries and central banks of five (later seven) major industrialized countries engaged in international trade and finance: Canada, France, Germany, Italy, Japan, the United Kingdom, and the United States.[1] This study is about the efforts of the Group of Five (G-5) and the Group of Seven (G-7) industrial countries to manage economic interdependence in the second half of the 1980s. It describes and evaluates the cooperative approach these countries have taken to the reduction of the large current account imbalances and currency misalignments that built up in the first half of the decade, in the hope of drawing lessons for the future.

The Meaning of Economic Policy Cooperation

Relations among national governments can be seen as ranging along a spectrum from open conflict to integration, where governments set policies jointly in a supranational forum to which they have ceded a large measure of authority (figure 1.1). At the midpoint of the spectrum lies policy indepen-

---

1. The countries are listed here in alphabetical order, following the convention in the G-7 communiqués. The tables and figures in this book, however, follow the IMF practice of grouping first the three non-European countries together, and then the European group.

FIGURE 1.1   The policy conflict–independence–integration spectrum

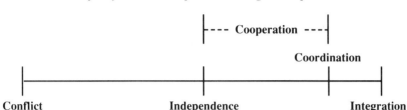

dence, in which governments simply take the policies of other governments as given, attempting neither to influence them nor be influenced by them. Between independence and integration lie coordination—joint problem identification and pursuit of mutually beneficial ways of tackling objectives—and (nearer the midpoint) a variety of forms of cooperation, such as information exchange, consultation, and mutual encouragement to adopt certain strategies or policies.

International coordination of economic decision making is the central theoretical concept in this study. Wallich (1984) provided the classic definition of coordination as a form of international interaction that produces " ... a significant modification of national policies in recognition of international economic interdependence." This definition can be used as a benchmark to evaluate the extent to which governments altered their policies either in response to pressure from other governments or in recognition of the consequences of spillovers.

In using this definition, however, it must be kept in mind that coordination does not extend to the government in question actually giving precedence to international over domestic concerns. In the theoretical literature on policy coordination, nations are assumed to engage in macroeconomic policy games in which each pursues its own aims, trading off changes in its own policies for policy changes by the others. Coordination is thus a way of expanding the choices available to national policymakers, by giving each government partial control over other governments' policy instruments.[2] That most of the countries examined here actually enjoyed robust growth with low inflation

---

2. Peter Kenen (1990) makes this point, citing Eichengreen (1985) and Buiter and Eaton (1985).

for most of the period in question suggests that the assumption that governments pursued their own rather than collective aims is valid for purposes of this analysis. Had there not been sustainable growth, one would have to deal with the possibility that some countries sacrificed some of their own potential prosperity for the common good.

The theoretical literature has provided useful analytical insights into the gains from coordination, the importance of governmental credibility, and other aspects of the international dealings of governments. At the same time, however, it must be acknowledged that the literature's focus on the pursuit of individual national goals has tended to ignore the fact that much international cooperation did indeed involve the definition and pursuit of agreed collective goals—what Marris (1986, 56) calls the "global objective."[3] A British veteran of the process, Sir Geoffrey Littler, in differentiating coordination from cooperation, has pointed out that a psychological shift occurs—to a common commitment, the definition of common aims from the outset, and a sense that the whole is greater than the parts, which goes beyond the search for common denominators among individual national aims (personal communication).

Certain other distinctions are also important to an understanding of the practice of coordination. One is the distinction between coordination of exchange rate policy and coordination of macroeconomic policy. Governments may adopt a goal of exchange rate stability and (as the Western European governments are committing themselves to do in the European Monetary System, or EMS) agree to discipline other areas of policy, particularly monetary policy, to achieve and maintain that goal. Alternatively, policymakers may decide to coordinate macroeconomic policies, agreeing to set such goals as the reduction of current account imbalances and employing fiscal and monetary policy and changes in exchange rates in pursuit of such goals. The distinction between exchange rate and macroeconomic policy coordination might seem a minor one, but as this study will show, the choice between them has become the central operational decision in deciding *how to coordinate economic policies internationally.*

Another important distinction is in the degree of automaticity with which policy changes are carried out. For example, a rules-based exchange rate system requires automatic changes in policy to maintain the exchange rate

---

3. This important point is also made by Kenen (1986).

objective. In contrast, a discretionary policy bargain produces mutual commitments that could achieve the same objective but allows governments to determine at what point action must be taken.

In the second half of the 1980s, these distinctions underlay differences in interpretations of coordination by the seven governments in ways that reduced the effectiveness of the process. Some preferred a system based on management of exchange rates, and these governments accorded the goal of exchange rate stability heavy weight and sought automatic policy changes to achieve that objective. Others preferred a discretionary, macroeconomic policy–based form of coordination, in a medium-term analytical framework, that would allow for application of the full range of supply- and demand-side policy instruments, including allowing the exchange rate to move.

These differences reflect differences among governments both with respect to objectives and with respect to analytical economic relationships—that is, how the global economy works. Those authorities who prefer exchange rate–based coordination tend to be more tolerant of government intervention in the economy. They believe that exchange rate variability is costly to real economic activity, and they have sought to reform the international monetary system to promote exchange rate stability. Those who prefer the more discretionary, medium-term approach reflect the market-oriented consensus that emerged in the 1980s to deal with uncertainties generated by economic shocks and changes in economic relationships. As might be expected, and as this study will illustrate in detail, these differing interpretations and objectives affected the manner in which coordination was carried out.

Plan of the Study

The next chapter offers a brief exposition of certain aspects of the theory of international policy coordination and the history of efforts to coordinate policy since World War II. Similarities and differences among governments are outlined in chapter 3, which summarizes the economic philosophies of the G-7 governments in recent years as well as the differing institutional mandates and organizational structures of their treasuries and central banks. Chapter 4 turns to the analytical framework that was constructed for the process of G-5 and G-7 coordination in the second half of the 1980s. This chapter shows how that process—organized around the economic summits and the meetings of ministers, central bankers, and deputies—actually worked, and illustrates the effects of national differences on the actual practice of coordination. The description in chapter 4 also stresses the informal nature of coordination as practiced in the G-7 and the influence individual personalities can have in the absence of an agreed framework for analysis and policy implementation.

What, then, did the G-7 participants accomplish through this process? This is the subject of chapter 5. Broadly speaking, economic performance has improved since 1985: current account imbalances have narrowed, fiscal policies in the major countries have changed in desirable directions, and exchange rates were less variable between 1987 and 1989 than in the years immediately preceding. The impact of the G-7 process itself on these changes is difficult to quantify, however. It would be fair to say in summary that true coordination was practiced in particular episodes: the Plaza Agreement, the Louvre Accord, and the "telephone accord" of late 1987. At other times, the process can better be described as mere cooperation rather than coordination, although it did succeed in influencing domestic policy debates in some tangible ways—through the use of foreign pressure (*gaiatsu*) in Japan, for example—and has contributed to a greater awareness of prudent policy in treasuries and has generated greater interest in microeconomic reform. The process has also achieved some intangible results by heading off crises.

Recommendations to strengthen the G-7 framework and process are presented in chapter 6. Although the process has lapsed into firefighting in recent years, it is not time to call for a requiem for policy coordination; rather, it is argued, we have heard only the prologue. There is too great a potential in the existing G-7 structure to allow it to lapse. Yet too little is being invested in system maintenance. Building on the analysis and diagnoses of the preceding chapters, chapter 6 offers five proposals:

- Involve central bankers more closely;
- Integrate exchange rate and macroeconomic policy considerations;
- Create an institutional memory and support by building a better defined professional base;
- Strengthen the mechanisms for implementing remedial policies;
- Rationalize the process by reducing the number of participants.

To set the stage for analysis in subsequent chapters, the next chapter outlines the framework implicit in that analysis and illustrates through a historical survey how the enthusiasm of authorities for cooperative arrangements and reform of the international monetary system has waxed and waned throughout the postwar period.

2 The Rationale and Recent History of Economic Policy Coordination

The Pros and Cons of Coordination

The basic logic of economic policy coordination is that, in an increasingly integrated world, the policies of one government can spill over to affect the goals of others, and therefore governments should consult one another and attempt to coordinate their actions so as to take these linkages into account. They should then be better off than if they had acted independently.

As policymakers gave greater attention to the shared problems of exchange rate variability, external imbalances, and Third World debt in the 1980s, economic theorists also began to focus their analyses on the study of coordination. These theorists have attempted to analyze the costs and benefits of coordination with the use of game theory models that incorporate the shared and conflicting interests of policymakers in different countries. This large literature has generated empirical estimates of the net gains from coordination (usually called "cooperation" in this literature) and has developed insights into both the possible gains and the costs.[1] The purely theoretical studies conclude that policy coordination is indeed worth pursuing in principle. The results of empirical analysis, on the other hand, are mixed and depend on the assumptions and structure of the model employed.

In the literature, the hypothetical gains from coordination can be diminished by very real costs. One set of costs arises from differences in and uncertainties about how economies work—how the effects of policies in one country really affect the goals of its partners, for instance. These uncertain-

---

1. This literature includes Currie et al. (1989), Horne and Masson (1988), Oudiz and Sachs (1984), and McKibbin and Sachs (forthcoming, 1991).

ties and differences give rise to the risk that governments will end up coordinating the wrong policies.

Most theoretical and empirical studies assume that information is freely available to the authorities and that a consensus exists about how the world economy operates. In reality, knowledge about linkages is still underdeveloped, forecasts are inaccurate, and unforeseen events throw off even the most sophisticated projections. Differences among countries with respect to objectives, economic structures, analytical methods used, national institutions, and political factors contribute to differing views among national authorities of how each other's economies and the world economy work. These differences can be costly. Frankel and Rockett (1988) have illustrated empirically how cooperative action based on the wrong model can produce a worse outcome than if governments acted independently.

Disagreements within countries—between treasuries and central banks, for example—about how domestic economies work are another important dimension of this problem. Such disagreements normally impede policy coordination, but they can also provide the basis for a coordinated policy package. For example, at the 1978 Bonn Summit (discussed later in this chapter), the negotiators were able to exploit domestic differences to enlist different domestic pressure groups in support of the various elements of the package.[2]

The transaction costs of negotiating and enforcing agreements are a second set of costs, and these can be substantial. Agreements take time to negotiate. At the Bonn Summit, the difficulties in arriving at a common analytical view that could also support a politically feasible agreement took so much time to overcome that, with the clarity of hindsight, it appears the policy package finally implemented actually overaccelerated the growth of aggregate demand.

National authorities may also change their plans after an agreement is reached and may renege or "cheat" on their commitments. Academic analysts using the game theory framework tend to treat this as a logical behavioral possibility, working it into the model rather than viewing it as a terminal event. Others have argued that governments are less likely to renege if they face credible threats of retaliation or peer pressure and surveillance. More likely is that governments may fail to deliver on policy commitments simply because they lack the political clout, will, or jurisdiction to do so, or

---

2. Putnam and Henning (1989, 98–114) develop this point in their analysis of the Bonn Summit.

because of internal differences over what to do.

Critics of coordination, however, question whether coordinated action really produces outcomes superior to those that might result from independent action. It has been argued that independent policymaking—particularly in the United States—could lead to better outcomes because the responsibility for policy change would then rest squarely where it belongs, with the executive and legislative branches. The empirical findings of Frankel and Rockett (1988) and Frankel (1984) led them to conclude that the gains from coordination are smaller than those from the US government following sensible policies on its own. Feldstein (1988a) has argued that coordination can provide undesirable opportunities for governments to obscure domestic paralysis about policy change and to try to shift the burden of adjustment abroad.[3] This argument is valid with respect to recent US behavior on some occasions, but whether such behavior achieves its aims depends as well on the willingness of other governments to accept an asymmetrical sharing of burdens. This they were willing to do at times in the period covered by this study.

Coordination in Recent History

Although these considerations can reduce the gains to coordination, coordination is generally assumed for purposes of analysis to be more worthwhile than pursuing independent national policies. That this assumption is widely shared is evidenced by the fact that governments have been groping toward cooperative arrangements during much of the postwar period. Policy coordination in the G-5 and G-7 is in fact the latest phase in an extensive history of international economic cooperation that reaches back to the 1920s and 1930s.

The central banks of the major industrial nations cooperated actively in the attempt during the interwar period to restore the gold standard, but countries subsequently proved reluctant to change their domestic policies to maintain it. Cooperation on monetary and trade policies broke down during the

---

3. Feldstein's view seems to have evolved somewhat since then; in an article in the *Financial Times* (Feldstein 1990), his recommendations to the G-7 hint of the need for an official view on exchange rate adjustment and of the possibility of coordinating fiscal and monetary policies.

competitive devaluations and protectionism of the Great Depression, but even during those bad times, governments pursued cooperative efforts.[4] Global cooperative arrangements in trade and finance were not revived, however, until after World War II, with the creation of the Bretton Woods institutions and the General Agreement on Tariffs and Trade (GATT).

Support for the Bretton Woods system derived from the determination of the Allies to prevent a recurrence of the self-defeating domestic policy measures associated with the breakdown of international cooperation during the Great Depression. At the same time, the International Monetary Fund (IMF) and the International Bank for Reconstruction and Development (the World Bank) were created as specialized agencies of the United Nations: the IMF to monitor and promote the stability of the international financial system created at Bretton Woods, and the World Bank to assist in postwar reconstruction and promote economic development globally.

In the Bretton Woods system, which lasted in its original form until 1973, countries agreed to a regime of fixed but adjustable exchange rates, in which currency relationships could be changed only if countries were in "fundamental disequilibrium," and then only with IMF approval. Governments were expected to adjust their economic policies to maintain the exchange rate objective, within balance of payments and reserves constraints, and were permitted to impose capital controls to handle unwanted capital outflows and inflows.

The 1944–73 period was not without episodes of noncooperation, however. Otmar Emminger (1984, 43), former President of the Deutsche Bundesbank, has described several instances where cooperation lapsed. For example, during the 1960s many Europeans (particularly the French) accused the United States of flooding the world with inflationary dollars; the Americans in turn charged that European failure to develop adequate capital markets was disturbing international financial equilibrium; and throughout the period several countries unilaterally revalued or devalued their currencies in violation of IMF discipline and at times even without consulting the IMF.

Increasing capital mobility, declining trade barriers in the wake of successive GATT negotiations, and advances in electronic and information technology all contributed in the 1960s and later to increasing the spillovers of domestic policies. The US balance of payments crisis in 1960 and 1961, for

---

4. For a more complete account of the interwar period see Fischer (1988).

example, gave rise to concerns about rising US direct investment in Europe and a debate about the implications for international inflation of the continuing US external deficit and relatively expansionary monetary policy.[5] During this period countries became less willing to play by the rules, as the need to subordinate domestic policy to international requirements asserted itself with increasing frequency.

These factors played a role in the failure of attempts to revive the Bretton Woods system in 1971 and 1972 and in its eventual demise in 1973. So did a persistent policy dilemma: ending the recurrent payments crises by which other countries met their reserve requirements might provoke a severe liquidity shortage, but there was also the danger of a crisis of confidence in the system if payments crises were allowed to recur. The dilemma was resolved by unilateral action by the Nixon administration in 1971, which led to setting the dollar afloat in 1973. Many have criticized the US action, but in retrospect it is difficult to see how the fixed exchange rate system could have withstood the large shocks, such as the 1973 oil price increase, that occurred not long thereafter.

Some of the major institutional arrangements for international cooperation that were developed during the last decade and a half of the Bretton Woods system continue to function today. One of these is the Bank for International Settlements (BIS), established in Basel, Switzerland, in 1930 as a central banks' bank. In its early years, the BIS had evolved into a mechanism for financial arrangements among the European countries, but in the early 1960s the US Federal Reserve System began to participate in its activities. Since then, the BIS has become a major forum for information exchange among the major central banks and for cooperation and coordination on international financial matters. The BIS also provides the secretariat for the Committee on Banking Regulations and Supervisory Practices (now known as the Basel Supervisors Committee), for the Board of Governors of the European Monetary Cooperation Fund, and for the Committee of EC Central Bank Governors.

Two other cooperative mechanisms—the Group of Ten and the so-called Working Party 3—had their origin at the Organization for Economic Cooperation and Development (OECD) in Paris. The Working Party 3 (WP3) of the OECD's Economic Policy Committee was created in 1961. As Crockett

---

5. Solomon (1982) provides a detailed account of this period.

(1989) has noted, the Bretton Woods founders anticipated the need for monetary cooperation to prevent competitive devaluations and beggar-thy-neighbor policies, but they did not foresee the need that arose for balance of payments adjustments. WP3 was intended to provide a mechanism that would promote cooperative management of adjustment, based on its analysis of and consultation on monetary, fiscal, and related policies. WP3 met very frequently in the 1960s and received solid analytical support from the OECD secretariat.

The Group of Ten (G-10) came into being in 1962 as part of the General Arrangements to Borrow to augment international liquidity at a time of rapid growth of world trade and output. In this forum, the treasury ministers and central bank governors of the 10 largest countries met to focus on systemic and institutional issues related to the expansion of liquidity, such as the management of Special Drawing Rights (SDRs) and IMF quotas.[6]

In the mid-1960s, a G-10 study of possible reforms of the international monetary system led to a request to WP3 to, in effect, report on policy guidelines for situations that seemed to pose balance of payments adjustment problems. Policymakers at the time were faced, as they were again in the 1980s, with the problem that major reserve-currency countries such as the United States and the United Kingdom were not prepared to pursue unilateral policies that would ensure balance of payments equilibrium. Nor were they prepared to change their exchange rates in instances of fundamental disequilibria.

WP3's report was published in 1966. It recognized that automatic adjustment mechanisms could not be relied upon to restore external equilibrium; instead, an institutional mechanism was required to develop policy guidelines and ensure that consultations were undertaken to encourage their implementation. The framework WP3 recommended is of interest here for its relevance to the later G-7 process. Chapter 4 will rely on that framework, drawing on Crockett (1989).

Despite the efforts of the G-10 and WP3, the Bretton Woods system did

---

6. The memberships of the G-10 and WP3 are essentially the same. The original G-10 included Belgium, Canada, France, Germany, Italy, Japan, the Netherlands, Sweden, the United Kingdom, and the United States, with observers from the international institutions. Switzerland was initially an observer, becoming a full member in 1984. In WP3, Belgium is part of the Dutch constituency, and Denmark and Norway share a seat with Sweden.

not survive, but interest in reviving a rule-based exchange rate system persisted. An early, unsuccessful attempt was made in 1974 by the Committee of Twenty (formally, the Committee on Reform of the International Monetary System and Related Issues, consisting of 20 members of the IMF). A study group convened by the independent international Group of Thirty in 1987 examined some of the reasons for this failure:

> Countries were not willing to accept the significant constraints of the Bretton Woods type of system where these conflicted with the macroeconomic policies they wished to pursue; and in any case flexible rates had become both increasingly respectable, certainly in academic circles, and increasingly unavoidable, given the growth of capital flows and divergent balance of payments pressures. With respect to the problem of international liquidity, the US was unwilling to participate in schemes which would build up the role of assets such as the SDR at the expense of the dollar; in any case a structural shift from asset to liability settlement was taking place. Other structural changes were also taking place, including a fundamental shift in the balance of power, with the growing importance of Europe and Japan, and the emergence of the ldc grouping. Finally, the significant economic shocks of the early 1970s, with their differential impact among economies, made it an unpropitious time to launch a new system. (Group of Thirty 1988, 11–12)

Efforts within Europe persisted, however, and in the early 1970s these produced the currency intervention arrangements known as the "snake," in which the EC central banks agreed to confine fluctuations among their currencies within a common margin of 2½ percent. These arrangements were superseded in 1979 by the launching of the EMS. Meanwhile, other governments expected that, with exchange rate flexibility to insulate them, they could pursue domestic policies without regard for spillovers and international consequences. Yet interdependence did not disappear with floating exchange rates. One reason was that countries were not indifferent to the international value of their currencies. Another was that the rapid structural changes that had undermined the Bretton Woods system continued to increase the incidence and impact of spillovers. The oil price shocks, for example, created sizeable external imbalances, which governments could only deal with effectively in a cooperative fashion. Yet cooperation remained limited and coordination, when it occurred, sporadic.

Several attempts to coordinate policy were made in and around the annual economic summits that were initiated in 1975. Concerns about economic performance and the desire for more formalized exchange rate arrangements motivated French President Valéry Giscard d'Estaing and German Chancellor

Helmut Schmidt to organize the first of these summits among the heads of state and of government from the largest industrial countries engaged in international trade.[7] In recent years the summit agendas have expanded to include a range of global issues, but in the 1970s summit participants devoted much of their attention to the performance of the world economy and how to improve it.

Economic performance at that time was not satisfactory. Rising inflation, recession, and unemployment plagued the industrial economies. After the 1973 oil shock, policy priorities shifted to coping with the impacts of the price shock and the need to avoid beggar-thy-neighbor policies. Use of Keynesian demand management policies was then still widely accepted, and fiscal stimulus became the favored instrument to move economic performance closer to potential.

Current account and inflation constraints made it obvious, however, that countries acting on their own could not solve the problem. The United States had been able to restore growth after the 1974–75 oil price shock and recession with a tax cut, but its current account and exchange rate were under first upward and then downward pressure. Part of the reason for the downward pressure lay with the US policy of maintaining the domestic oil price below world prices, which forestalled any reduction in domestic demand, reduced domestic supply, and thus contributed to a heavy oil import bill.

Germany, meanwhile, was deeply concerned about its growth prospects. Both Germany and Japan were running current account surpluses, which the United States felt provided a basis for more expansionary domestic macroeconomic policies in those countries. Germany resisted this prescription, but saw that its interest would be served if the United States would raise its domestic oil prices to world levels. The elements of a policy package seemed to exist.

The summit leaders considered a policy bargain to address unemployment and oil import dependence at successive summits in London in 1977 and Bonn in 1978. In London, the leaders were able to agree to growth objectives for themselves; when a year later they had failed to achieve these

---

7. In addition to France, Germany, Japan, the United Kingdom, and the United States, Italy was included in the 1975 summit as the result of a decision made during the preparatory meetings; Canada was invited in 1976 and the President of the European Commission in 1977.

objectives, they decided at the Bonn meeting to be more specific. In Bonn, Germany committed itself to increase its fiscal deficit by 1 percent of GNP, Japan to increase public spending if it failed to meet its growth target, and the United States to raise domestic oil prices to world levels; all participants undertook to complete the Tokyo Round of multilateral trade negotiations in the GATT by December 1978. All of these commitments were implemented.

The package adopted in Bonn meets most of the criteria for true policy coordination. Participants shared *ex ante* the objectives of the policy package, and extensive preparation lay behind it, so that governments subsequently felt bound by and honored their commitments. Yet the Bonn Summit has been criticized—even cited as a failure of coordination by some, including some of the participants—in the light of subsequent macroeconomic performance: inflation soared and was followed by the severe 1980–81 recession. However, the Bonn Summit was not a failure of coordination as defined. Indeed coordination worked pretty well. The problem was the poor timing of the agreed-upon policies, together with the totally unexpected oil shock that intervened in 1979.

The Bonn episode illustrates how the gains of coordination can be reduced by such factors as the length of time needed for negotiation. Students of the economic summits have argued that the critics of the Bonn agreement have been unfair: although the policy changes were indeed implemented as much as a year too late, no one could have foreseen the January 1979 oil price shock. These students hold that the expansionary fiscal policy changes agreed to at Bonn were only a marginal contributor to the inflation that followed.[8] In retrospect, it is also evident that monetary policies at the time were too expansionary—oil price shock or not.

Other cooperative episodes during the 1970s related to US initiatives to improve its international competitive position, as Bergsten (1986) has demonstrated. After the Nixon "shock" of August 1971, when the United States suspended gold convertibility and imposed a 10 percent import surcharge in pursuit of currency realignment, the Nixon administration began to take a more cooperative stance and late that year negotiated the Smithsonian Agreement. This agreement established a margin within which member currencies would fluctuate against the dollar. The Carter administration

---

8. See Putnam and Bayne (1987, chapters 4 and 5), Putnam and Henning (1989), and Gerald Holtham (1989) for a detailed analysis.

in late 1977 urged Japan and Germany, in what some saw as a unilateralist stance, to adopt growth-oriented policies to reduce an overvalued dollar. In 1978 it launched an international effort to support the dollar as it plummeted that year in response to accelerating US inflation and loss of confidence in the administration's policies.

In October 1979 the Federal Reserve changed the conduct of US monetary policy and adopted a more overt anti-inflation stance. Other central banks followed in an uncoordinated manner. As each central bank did what it thought best to reduce domestic inflation, the synchronization of monetary policy produced an aggregate restrictive effect that deepened the ensuing recession more than any single institution intended—or than might have occurred if they and their treasury counterparts had coordinated their policies.

Shortly thereafter, in 1982, government leaders at the Versailles Summit directed the G-5 treasury ministers to undertake multilateral surveillance of each other's domestic policies and their international implications. The Managing Director of the IMF was invited to participate in these discussions.[9] These arrangements were a compromise resulting from US resistance to French pressure for exchange rate stabilization and reform of the international monetary system. The leaders also requested that the treasury ministers and central bank governors prepare a report on the effectiveness of exchange market intervention. The study, actually prepared by the deputies of the treasury ministers and central bank governors and known as the Jurgensen Report after its chairman Philippe Jurgensen, was in some ways a prelude to the G-5 and G-7 policy coordination of the middle and late 1980s, and revealed the countries' differences over exchange market intervention.[10]

Following the election of President Ronald Reagan in 1980, the new US administration seemed to consider cooperative arrangements dispensable. More central to its concerns were the medium-term objectives of economic recovery and a reduction of the role of government in the economy. To achieve the latter objective, the Reagan administration and Congress adopted a fiscal package that was intended to reduce taxes and spending sharply.

---

9. See Putnam and Bayne (1987, 161) for an explanation of the rationale for the mandate and for the invitation to the IMF Managing Director to participate.

10. Another instance of policy cooperation in the early 1980s occurred in response to the emergence of the international debt crisis in mid-1982. Loose forms of cooperation involved the G-5, G-10, and other forums as well.

Since military spending was to be increased, however, total spending could only be reduced by squeezing other areas sufficiently to pay for both the growth in military spending and reduced tax rates. Instead of reallocating and reducing public spending, the structural deficit increased, creating a saving-investment imbalance and, as a result, a deterioration in the US external balance.

At this time, as in some earlier episodes such as the 1978 dollar support effort noted by Bergsten (1986), the external consequences of unilateral pursuit of US policy objectives required an international cooperative response if it was to be dealt with successfully. In this instance the cooperative response began with the G-5's Plaza Agreement in September 1985, which is where the detailed analysis of this study begins.

3   Institutions and Players

Despite the increasing integration of the world's major economies, the nation-state remains the basis for economic policy formation. The challenge for coordination is to identify, in the context of an ever-changing economic outlook, some basis for mutually beneficial policy change—to improve the economic prospects for all the countries involved, rather than undermine those prospects by working autonomously, and possibly at cross purposes.

National factors that influence the success of policy coordination include economic policies and philosophies; economic institutions and their mandates and relationships with each other and with their foreign counterparts; and the personalities and views of the leaders of those institutions. This chapter examines each of these factors to arrive at important implications for the coordination process with respect to the roles and tenure of key officials, jurisdictional overlaps, and the ability to deliver, at home, on policy commitments made in the international arena.

The term "players" is used here to refer to the individual policymakers—the treasury ministers,[1] the central bank governors, and senior treasury officials—in the G-7 countries. (Senior central bank officials have not been regular G-7 participants in the past.) Officials of the International Monetary Fund are also among the players, serving as objective outsiders and supplying the data and policy analysis that are essential to effective policy coordination. The players and their tenures in the process are arrayed in figure 3.1.

---

1. "Treasury" and "finance ministry" are terms used in different countries for what is essentially the same institution. Where appropriate, this study uses "treasury" as a generic term referring to the ministry in charge of macroeconomic and financial affairs.

FIGURE 3.1 **Participants in the G-5 and G-7 process and their tenures, 1985–89**

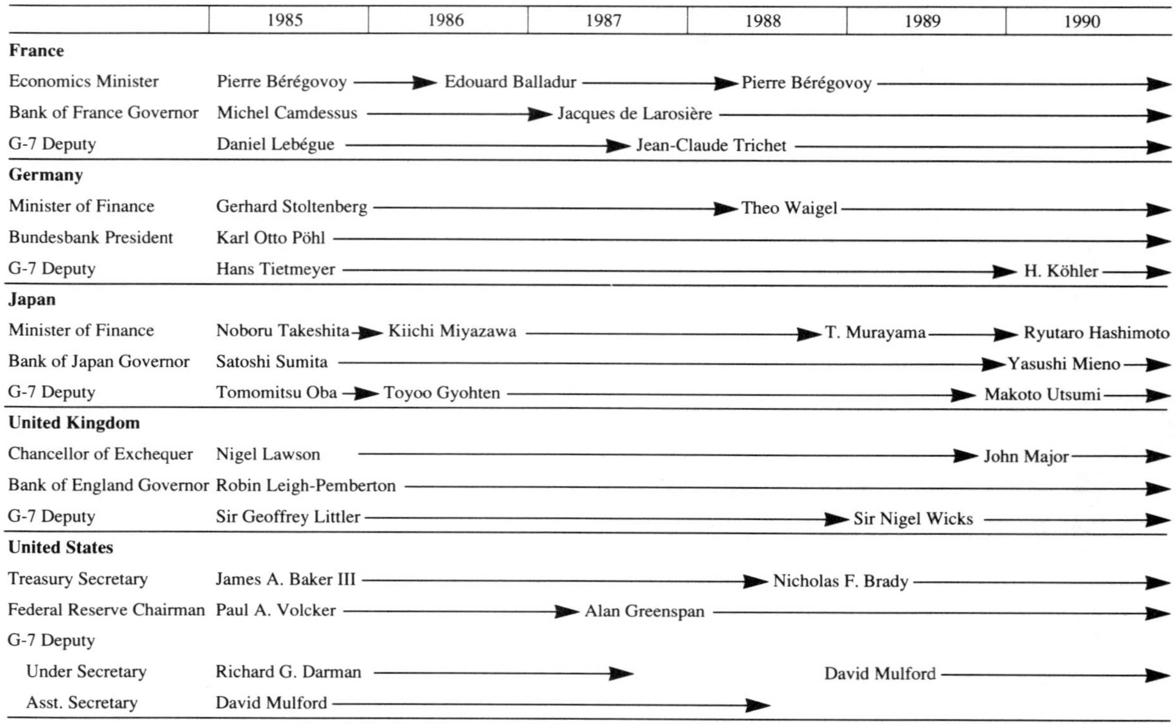

	1985	1986	1987	1988	1989	1990
France						
Economics Minister	Pierre Bérégovoy →	Edouard Balladur		→ Pierre Bérégovoy →		→
Bank of France Governor	Michel Camdessus →		→ Jacques de Larosière →			→
G-7 Deputy	Daniel Lebégue →		→ Jean-Claude Trichet →			→
Germany						
Minister of Finance	Gerhard Stoltenberg →			→ Theo Waigel →		→
Bundesbank President	Karl Otto Pöhl →					→
G-7 Deputy	Hans Tietmeyer →					→ H. Köhler
Japan						
Minister of Finance	Noboru Takeshita →	Kiichi Miyazawa →		→ T. Murayama →		→ Ryutaro Hashimoto
Bank of Japan Governor	Satoshi Sumita →					→ Yasushi Mieno
G-7 Deputy	Tomomitsu Oba →	Toyoo Gyohten →				→ Makoto Utsumi
United Kingdom						
Chancellor of Exchequer	Nigel Lawson →				→ John Major →	
Bank of England Governor	Robin Leigh-Pemberton →					→
G-7 Deputy	Sir Geoffrey Littler →			→ Sir Nigel Wicks →		→
United States						
Treasury Secretary	James A. Baker III →			→ Nicholas F. Brady →		→
Federal Reserve Chairman	Paul A. Volcker →		→ Alan Greenspan →			→
G-7 Deputy						
Under Secretary	Richard G. Darman →				→ David Mulford →	
Asst. Secretary	David Mulford →		→			

FIGURE 3.1 Participants in the G-5 and G-7 process and their tenures, 1985–89 (continued)

	1985	1986	1987	1988	1989	1990
Canada[a]						
Minister of Finance			Michael Wilson ─────────────────────▶			
Bank of Canada Governor			John Crow ──────────────────────────▶			
G-7 Deputy			[b] ──────▶ Wendy Dobson ──────────▶ David Dodge ──▶			
Italy[a]						
Minister of the Treasury			[c] ────────▶ Giuliano Amato ─▶ Guido Carli ──▶			
Bank of Italy Governor			Carlo Ciampi ───────────────────────▶			
G-7 Deputy			Mario Sarcinelli ───────────────────▶			
International Monetary Fund						
Managing Director	Jacques de Larosière ───────▶ Michel Camdessus ──▶					
Economic Counsellor			Jacob A. Frenkel ───────────────────▶			
Key Events	P	To	L V Te	E		

P = Plaza Agreement; To = Tokyo Summit; L = Louvre Accord; V = Venice Summit; Te = "telephone summit"; E = US presidential election.

a. Representatives from Italy and Canada were invited to join the Louvre ministerial meeting. Although the Italian delegation traveled to Paris for the meeting, Finance Minister Giovanni Goria decided not to participate because he had not participated in the preparatory discussions.

b. Bernard Drabble was the Canadian G-7 deputy in the first half of 1987.

c. Giovanni Goria was the Italian Finance Minister from the time of the Louvre meeting in February until the spring of 1987.

National Economic Policies and Philosophies

Governments' broad economic policy objectives—economic growth, high employment, price stability, and balance of international payments—have not changed much in the postwar period, but their relative importance and the means used to achieve them have.[2] These changes in the weight of objectives and the choice of instruments reflect overall national goals, economic policy preferences, and foreign economic policy objectives. An understanding of such changes in turn helps to explain and predict countries' interest in imposing these preferences on others in international bargaining, and their willingness to coordinate—that is, to modify their own policies in recognition of growing international interdependence.

Countries' policy preferences, for employment growth or tolerance of inflation, for example, have been influenced by their historical experience. As a result of Germany's experience with hyperinflation in the 1920s, the German public places heavy emphasis on price stability as a key economic objective (but has been able to achieve high rates of growth and employment in much of the postwar period nonetheless). The historical experience of the United Kingdom, the United States, and Canada, on the other hand, has included high unemployment during the interwar period and to a lesser extent at times in the postwar period; this experience has contributed to a greater tolerance of inflation.

A country's external economic policy objectives are a function of such factors as economic size and dependence on international transactions for its economic welfare. Large, relatively closed economies such as the United States and Japan, where international trade has accounted for a relatively small proportion of total output and consumption, have tended to be less sensitive to the consequences of their domestic policies for the international trade and financial system. More open economies such as Canada and the United Kingdom have traditionally placed considerable emphasis on the promotion of liberal trade and free capital movements. The United States, despite having a more closed economy, has taken much responsibility for systemic issues of world security in the postwar period, and has willingly provided leadership and resources to promote trade liberalization. This view

---

2. More extensive surveys of national economic and political factors and their impact on international relations include those by Bergsten (1975, 20–45) and Katzenstein (1978).

has contrasted with those of Japan, which has pursued its objective of rapid modernization in a mercantilist fashion, and France, which has been relatively protectionist.

The 1960s and part of the 1970s were characterized by policy activism in pursuit of economic objectives, as described by Polak:

> During this period of policy activism the authorities were, on the whole, successful in keeping two of their economic policy objectives, growth and employment, on track although it should be noted that with respect to the latter, policy had already become less ambitious than it had been in the immediate postwar years. . . . The authorities were less successful in dealing with the balance of payments and, from the early 1970s onward, inflation. To keep the indicators of their domestic policy objectives within a narrow range, governments were quite prepared to make frequent adjustments in their policy instruments . . . they were, however, quite hesitant to use the exchange rate to remedy wide divergences in the current account . . . from its target of approximate balance. . . . The sharp distinction between objectives (or targets) as variables about which we care, and instruments as variables about which we do not care, was still *grosso modo* true at that time. . . . (Polak 1988, 5)

This period of policy activism saw the adoption of different national economic strategies in response to such external shocks as the 1973 oil price increase. These strategies can be thought of as arrayed on a spectrum, with the relatively market-oriented approaches of the United States and the United Kingdom at one end, the more interventionist orientations of Japan and France at the other end, and the strategies of the other three governments in between.

In the late 1970s, however, a marked shift occurred in the economic philosophies of most OECD governments. This change affected both their goals and their instruments. Short-term demand management strategies came under increasing challenge as governments struggled to reduce persistent high inflation, contain large public-sector deficits incurred in the 1970s, and remove numerous growth-constraining rigidities. Governments increasingly accepted that their role was to unleash the growth potential of the private sector and to confine themselves to framework policies involving medium-term settings for monetary and fiscal policy. Although trade and industrial policies continued to reflect differing degrees of market orientation, macroeconomic policies tended during the 1980s to converge on a medium-term approach to sustained growth with low inflation. Polak characterizes this change in thinking as follows:

> The two major changes . . . the reordering among objectives and the reordering between objectives and instruments—are obviously interrelated. Most strikingly, the downgrading of unemployment as a primary concern of economic policy reflects at the same time the disenchantment with incomes policy as an instrument to reduce the price component, and raise the output component, of a specified increase in money GDP. (Polak 1988, 5)

Within this overall reorientation, however, objectives were weighted differently from country to country, and the instruments used to achieve them differed as well. Not unexpectedly, these factors helped to explain the views and approaches countries brought to the coordination process in the second half of the 1980s, as later chapters will describe. In Japan, for example, robust economic growth remained a major goal in the 1980s (as it had been for the more than 120 years during which Japan sought to catch up with the West), and one that Japan has successfully pursued since 1975 without protracted periods of high inflation. Japan has been able to retain flexibility with respect to demand management, although the need for fiscal consolidation was a constraining factor in the latter half of the 1980s. Japan's success as an exporter of manufactured goods has also contributed to its excellent economic growth record, but has brought increasing trade frictions with the United States and the European Community in the 1980s. *Gaiatsu*, or the use of foreign pressure, has had some effectiveness in opening Japanese markets to imports and in persuading the Japanese to loosen certain regulatory restrictions that served the interests of domestic producer groups. The importance the Japanese attach to harmonious international relations has also played a role in bringing these changes about.

Economic growth has also been a major goal in France, which embarked on a "dash for growth" in 1982. The Socialist government's expansionary fiscal policy soon produced an external crisis, however, and was replaced by a medium-term growth plan aimed at lowering unit costs of production to below those in Germany. The franc was effectively pegged to the deutsche mark. Extensive adjustment occurred in the real economy as flexibility was restored through fiscal consolidation, privatization, and deregulation. The resulting economic policy discipline is part of an overall strategy to build the credibility necessary to support French ambitions for leadership in shaping future economic arrangements in Europe.

The United States, Canada, Italy, and the United Kingdom have also made restoring and sustaining economic growth a primary goal since the 1981–82 recession, but these countries have had to pay attention to containing inflationary pressures as well. The United States had the most consistent success of the four in maintaining inflation at moderate levels in the 1980s. In the wake of the Federal Reserve's anti-inflation strategy begun in 1979, the Reagan administration eschewed reflation during and after the severe 1980–81 recession. Inflation remained moderate, thanks in part to the decline in oil prices in 1986, and unemployment declined as a result of an expansionary fiscal policy, the relaxation of monetary policy, and increased wage flexibility. But the Reagan administration's goal of reducing the size of government through tax cuts and reduced spending misfired; large increases in military spending were not matched by similar spending cuts elsewhere. The resulting fiscal expansion and underlying saving-investment imbalance contrasted with the fiscal consolidation achieved in Germany and Japan and resulted in large current account imbalances and misalignment of the US dollar against the yen and the mark.

Canada, Italy, and the United Kingdom had greater difficulty in restraining inflation as they pursued their growth objectives, but for different reasons. Canada's inflation rate dropped in the early 1980s in the face of the most severe recession in the industrialized countries. Like Italy, however, Canada had a large and persistent fiscal deficit; this and resurgent cost pressures contributed by the end of the decade to high interest rates, sluggish growth, and a large current account deficit. The United Kingdom, in contrast, moved into public-sector surplus in the 1980s as a result of the medium-term economic strategy adopted in the 1980–81 budget. Although monetary policy was tightened to reduce inflation, it was also the preferred instrument, rather than fiscal policy, to respond to short-term economic developments. Credit market deregulation in the mid-1980s contributed to a consumption boom in subsequent years; loosening of monetary policy associated with pursuit of an exchange rate target in 1987–88 and reduction of personal tax rates contributed to a resurgence of inflation and a current account deficit at the end of the decade.

Germany has traditionally accorded considerable weight to low inflation as both a domestic and an international objective. Widespread public support for this goal has meant a willingness to sacrifice growth objectives and contain cost pressures if necessary in the quest for price stability. Growth has also fallen short of potential because of extensive regulation and subsidization, adopted as part of the pursuit of equity in the social market economy of the 1960s and early 1970s. Until political events in the German Democratic

Republic in late 1989 led to costly reunification plans, fiscal consolidation was pursued by the West German government as part of a "supply-side" strategy to restore growth momentum and economic flexibility.

National Economic Institutions and Their Leaders

The national economic institutions responsible for managing interdependence in the seven major industrial countries are the treasuries and the central banks. The manner of their participation in international policymaking is influenced by national economic strategies; by the relative mandates of the treasury, the central bank, and other ministries with responsibility for economic policy; by the role of the private sector in policymaking; and by the degree of concentration of power to make and fulfill international commitments. These national differences are crucial to an understanding of the evolution of policy coordination in the 1980s. They contributed to the coordination of macroeconomic policy change in some countries and constrained it in others; they influenced views about exchange rate management and about the coordination process itself. Differences in substantive focus and in political independence among treasuries, central banks, and other economic ministries also had important implications for policy cooperation.

THE TREASURIES AND TREASURY MINISTERS

Each national treasury must carry forward the objectives of its political masters, using expenditure and taxation policies, debt management, international economic relations, regulatory relationships with domestic financial institutions, the formulation of exchange rate policy in some cases, and (in three countries) the formulation of monetary policy. In some countries the treasury must share responsibility for economic policy with other ministries.

The mandates and powers of treasuries thus vary in breadth and depth. Table 3.1 summarizes the roles of the G-7 treasuries in decision making, execution, and consultation with respect to several policy areas that are key to the coordination process (areas, such as tax policy, that have primarily domestic impacts are excluded).

The UK Treasury has the broadest reach. Its head, the Chancellor of the Exchequer, has responsibility for proposing overall economic strategy to the

TABLE 3.1 Powers of the G-7 treasuries[a]

Country	Fiscal policy	Monetary policy	Exchange rate policy	Foreign exchange market intervention[b]	Financial market regulation	Structural Reform
Canada	D, E	C	D, E/C	C	D, E, C	D/C
Japan	D, E, C	D, C	D, C	D, C	D, E, C	E, C[c]
United States	C	C	D, E/C	D, C	D, E, C	
France	D, E, C	D/C	D, C	C	D, E, C	D/C[d]
Germany	D, E, C	C	D, C[e]	C	D/C	C
Italy	D/C, E	D/C	D, E/C	C	D, E, C	
United Kingdom	D, E, C	D, C	D, E, C	C	D, C	D/C[f]

C = consultative role only; D = decision-making power; E = execution/implementation powers; D/C = decision-making power in consultation with other agencies; E/C = execution/implementation in consultation with other agencies.

a. Judgments are based on interpretation of the exercise of *de jure* mandates.

b. France, Germany, Italy, and the United Kingdom are members of the exchange rate mechanism (ERM) of the European Monetary System; foreign-exchange market intervention by their central banks is in accord with ERM commitments. The consultation procedures vary from country to country.

c. The Ministry of Finance is responsible for operating the Fiscal Investment and Loan Program, which channels savings from pension funds and the postal savings system into construction projects through loans at both market and preferential rates.

d. The treasury plays a major role in identification and formulation of structural reform.

e. Under a floating exchange rate regime, final decisions on foreign-exchange market intervention lie with the Bundesbank. Exchange rate realignments in the EMS are the responsibility of the Finance Ministry.

f. The Treasury plays a major role in identification and formulation of structural reforms.

cabinet; for the conduct of fiscal, monetary, and tax policy; and for international financial affairs. The French Ministry of Economy, Finance, and the Budget (of which the Trésor is a part) has a similarly broad reach, with responsibility for the budget, taxation, financial market regulation, and (at least at certain times in the past) privatization, and a heavy emphasis on international economic affairs: for example, it provides the chair and the secretariat for the Paris Club process that manages the rescheduling of Third World official debt.

Canada's Minister of Finance has overall responsibility for promoting the functioning of the economy. This mandate involves a broad economic oversight role and direct responsibility for the conduct of budget and taxation policy, regulation of financial markets, and conduct of international financial affairs. The minister also has certain trade policy responsibilities, particularly with respect to imports.

In contrast, treasuries in the United States, Japan, and Germany must share responsibility for economic policy with other ministries. The US Treasury shares policymaking responsibilities with the Congress and with other agencies in the executive branch. The Treasury's domestic policy responsibilities include tax policy, revenue collection, aspects of financial market regulation, and debt management. It shares responsibility for economic projections and strategy (where the Council of Economic Advisers has lead responsibility), and for the annual budget (for which the Office of Management and Budget has the lead). Likewise in international financial affairs, allocation of responsibilities among US agencies is not without ambiguity. US law grants both the Treasury and the Federal Reserve the right to intervene in foreign-exchange markets. Although the former argues that it is first among equals in exchange rate policy determination, this legal point remains unresolved. The Fed, however, because it is independent in domestic monetary policymaking and is deeply involved in financial issues, has considerable clout, whatever the legal ambiguities. Thus, the two bureaucracies cooperate closely with regard to intervention.[3]

---

3. A detailed analysis of jurisdictions as they are exercised in U.S. exchange rate policymaking can be found in Destler and Henning (1989).

The Japanese and German ministries of finance have more exclusive mandates than the US Treasury for budget and taxation policy, but each shares responsibility with other ministries for such international economic strategy and medium-term issues as structural reform: in Germany with the Economics Ministry and in Japan with the Economic Planning Agency and the Ministry of International Trade and Industry (MITI). The Japanese Ministry of Finance has lead authority for financial market regulation, whereas in Germany this responsibility is shared with the central bank, the Bundesbank. In Italy, the Ministry of the Treasury has de jure responsibility for budget policy and for setting the discount rate.

THE CENTRAL BANKS

The mandates of the central banks, and hence their relationships with the treasuries, vary across a wide spectrum of independence from political pressure (as can be inferred from the columns for monetary and exchange rate policy and foreign-exchange market intervention in table 3.1). All the central banks, however, have the maintenance of domestic price stability as a central, if not exclusive, objective, whereas most treasuries are given responsibility for multiple objectives. At one end of the independence spectrum is the Deutsche Bundesbank, which has a clear legislative mandate of independence in its conduct of monetary policy and foreign-exchange market intervention. The German Finance Ministry determines policy with respect to the exchange rate system, such as participation in the EMS. It maintains a close consultative role with the Bundesbank, and conflict between the two rarely surfaces in public. The Central Bank Council, consisting of the Bundesbank Directorium and the presidents of the central banks of the individual German states, or Länder, plays an important role in determining the Bundesbank's monetary and credit policies. Representatives of the government may also attend the Central Bank Council's meetings.

The Bank of England, the Bank of Japan, and the Bank of France lie at the other end of the spectrum, with more limited independence. Monetary policy and exchange rate decisions in the United Kingdom are made by the Chancellor of the Exchequer after a consultative process that begins with middle-level officials of the Bank of England and the Treasury and culminates, after meetings with senior officials of both institutions and the Governor of the Bank of England, by informing the Prime Minister of the intended action.

Although the Bank of Japan Act stipulates central bank independence in formulating interest rate policy, in practice the bank's Governor obtains the government's agreement to interest rate changes before they are carried into action. The Ministry of Finance also firmly controls exchange rate policy formulation, but it relies on the Bank of Japan for execution. In France, under existing legislation decisions are made through a consultive process between the Governor and the treasury minister, although French authorities have indicated from time to time an intention to make the Bank an independent entity.

The US Federal Reserve is situated toward the independent end of the spectrum: its independence in the formulation and conduct of monetary policy is expressly provided for in US law. The US Treasury has responsibility for formulating exchange rate policy, but the Fed has independent legal authority to operate in foreign-currency markets, and it acts as the executing agent for the Treasury in these markets. Effective exercise of these split jurisdictions depends heavily on close consultation and good personal relations among senior officials in the two institutions.[4] The Bank of Canada is situated on the independence spectrum near the Fed, but somewhat toward the center. The Bank of Italy is also located toward this end of the spectrum by virtue of its history of strong leadership and staff.

The central banks' exercise of their mandates is, of course, influenced by the personal characteristics of their governors and senior officials. Strong, experienced, and well-respected central bank leaders often exert a sway over economic affairs well beyond their de jure authority. The central banks of England, Japan, and France have all known periods of considerable de facto freedom in the exercise of monetary and exchange rate policy, despite their formal constraints.

THE G-7 DEPUTIES

In each of the seven treasuries, one senior official is designated as responsible for international affairs, including representation of the ministry in G-7 proceedings below the ministerial level. There they are charged with advising on and monitoring the other countries' economic performance, and with

---

4. See the concluding chapter in Destler and Henning (1989).

conducting bargaining on remedial policy actions. In the most immediate sense, it is through the deputies that national viewpoints and demands are brought to bear on both the diagnosis and the prescription of cooperative policies.

The positions and responsibilities of the G-7 deputies in the national treasuries differ from country to country, but most are responsible for certain other areas of policy as well, including in most cases financial affairs, and most rank very near the top of their departments. Few have direct responsibilities for domestic economic or fiscal affairs. The rationale for this limitation may be a practical one: these officials spend so much time on international issues (which often require international travel) that little time remains for other responsibilities. But the consequence, as we shall see, can be an artificial separation of domestic and international goals that is counterproductive to managing interdependence.

Since the second Reagan administration, the US G-7 deputy has been an Assistant Secretary or an Under Secretary of the Treasury (the latter is the more senior position) who is responsible for international monetary affairs, including foreign-exchange market intervention, and who reports directly to the Secretary of the Treasury. Certain domestic responsibilities held by previous under secretaries were reallocated elsewhere in the second Reagan administration. Taxation and domestic treasury functions fall under other officers of similar rank in the Treasury; macroeconomic policy responsibilities are shared with the Council of Economic Advisers, the Office of Management and Budget, and the Federal Reserve, as described above.

In Japan, Germany, France, and Italy, deputies' relationships with the minister and departmental responsibilities are broadly similar. The Japanese Vice Minister (International) reports directly to the Minister of Finance, from a position near the apex of the bureaucratic pyramid. This, however, is a staff position, which relates very closely with the Bureau of International Finance and the international sides of the banking and security bureaus. Traditionally, the Japanese G-7 deputy also plays an important diplomatic role for the Ministry of Finance.

In Germany, two state secretaries (Staatssekretar) in the Finance Ministry report directly to the minister. One of these acts as Germany's G-7 deputy and carries responsibility for the international functions of the ministry and for financial market affairs; the other has responsibility for the budget and for taxation. Unlike in the United States and Japan, however, the responsibility for foreign-exchange market intervention lies with the Bundesbank. In

France, the international responsibilities of the ministry are directed by the Director of the Treasury (Directeur du Trésor); a similar position exists on the budget side of the ministry as well. Both report directly to the minister. In Italy, the Director General of the Ministry of the Treasury carries major responsibility for domestic and international financial affairs, reporting directly to the minister.

In Canada and the United Kingdom responsibilities are allocated and exercised differently. In the United Kingdom, the Second Permanent Secretary of Her Majesty's Treasury has primary responsibility for international economic affairs and for financial markets; he works directly with the Chancellor of the Exchequer but reports to him through the Permanent Secretary. Policymaking responsibility is shared with the Chief Economist, who is involved in all aspects of policy including monetary and exchange rate policy. In Canada, the situation is similar: the G-7 role is carried out by one of two associate deputy ministers working directly with the Minister of Finance but reporting to him through the Deputy Minister. This Associate Deputy also has certain domestic macroeconomic responsibilities.

The International Monetary Fund

Since the early 1980s, surveillance of economic performance by the G-5 and G-7 has been conducted with the assistance of the Managing Director of the IMF. This participation has been personal and informal. The views of the Managing Director are sought as those of a technical expert, but also as an objective referee and a representative of the economic interests of the rest of the world. A senior member of the IMF staff, the Economic Counsellor and Director of Research, has worked closely with the deputies in the definition and development of economic indicators used in surveillance and as an economic adviser.

The IMF has been important in maintaining the rigor of G-5 and G-7 surveillance, since it is expected to place global economic welfare above the particular national interests of the participants. Its representatives provide the analytical tools necessary for disinterested assessment of the external implications of participants' existing policies and of changing those policies. Since personnel at the national level frequently change, for a variety of reasons, the IMF representatives also give valuable continuity to the exercise, by providing and preserving the objective framework for surveillance.

Implications and Conclusions

Convergence of national economic strategies and an increasing awareness of international linkages have diminished the obstacles to the pursuit of common policy objectives, but differences in decision-making mandates and the lack of congruence between the international responsibilities and the domestic authority of some of the major players continue to throw up obstacles to effective coordination. Three important sets of problems are those affecting the roles and responsibilities of the G-7 deputies, jurisdictional issues, and institutional problems affecting the ability of countries to deliver on their commitments. Two additional problems are the high rate of personnel turnover observed in senior positions, alluded to above, and (at the international rather than the national level) the restricted role assigned to the IMF in the coordination process.

THE ROLE OF THE TREASURY DEPUTIES

The multilateral economic analysis that underpins the G-7's policy discussions and decisions is carried out by the treasury deputies. Yet few of the deputies have direct macroeconomic policy responsibilities, and therefore few have control over the macroeconomic instruments over which they engage in international policy bargaining. (In some cases their ministers lack this power as well.) Likewise, few deputies have direct responsibility for the analytical work that is required for the policy coordination exercise to function; macroeconomic projections and modeling, for example, are usually carried out by units responsible for fiscal policy or economic planning. It thus becomes difficult for deputies to provide the appropriate analytical input to an international forum when they are not responsible for generating that analysis at home. Finally, most deputies have some responsibilities for financial affairs; the main policy instrument over which some have direct control is foreign-exchange market intervention. This configuration of responsibilities can create a preference for use of the intervention instrument over other policy instruments.

JURISDICTIONAL PROBLEMS

As the variation in central bank independence across countries implies, tensions between treasuries and central banks over the conduct of macroeconomic policy can be expected to surface in the coordination debate. Just as the way these tensions are addressed and resolved is important for market confidence in domestic policies, so it is for international policy coordination as well. If central bankers are focused on long-run domestic price stability, it is unlikely that they will be willing to change that focus to achieve short-run exchange rate objectives, especially if the two conflict.

Even where treasuries and central banks are able to agree on the action to be taken, their divided jurisdictions, particularly in the key currency countries, can also complicate cooperation with respect to intervention in exchange markets. In the three largest countries, the treasuries are responsible for exchange rate policy, but their responsibilities and powers for intervention differ. In Germany, the Bundesbank is independent of the Finance Ministry in this regard. Communication on intervention issues with other treasuries, mainly the US Treasury, has to observe these jurisdictional responsibilities; this can mean that communications have to be indirect, either through the Federal Reserve to the Bundesbank or through the German Finance Ministry to the Bundesbank.

This division of jurisdictions, particularly in the United States and Germany, also means that the will to cooperate across agency boundaries can be as important to the success of coordination as any factor in the international framework. Students of summitry have provided a number of anecdotes showing how views have indeed differed across these agencies. Public accounts in the US press during the 1985–89 period have likewise confirmed the existence of both differences of view (most evident in the regular public criticism by administration officials of the Fed's views about inflation risks, and Fed criticism of the Treasury concerning intervention) and difficulties of communication.

ABILITY TO DELIVER

The diffusion of decision-making power in the United States has made it difficult for US participants to deliver on commitments made in the coordination process. Fiscal policymaking is constrained by the diffusion of responsibility between the legislative and executive branches. But as Kenen (1988) has pointed out, the problem is not constitutional but political. The paralysis is not permanent, but it can go on for a long time. Breaking it depends on the ability and commitment of the leadership in both branches to build a domestic coalition for policy change.

Political constraints on Germany's role in burden sharing have also had an impact on coordination. German resistance to fiscal stimulus in favor of structural changes since the late 1970s has gradually won the agreement of some other participants, but ironically the German government has been slow to deliver on these changes. Funabashi (1989) has described political factors in the German coalition government that might account for this; for example, the Economics Ministry, which is largely responsible for structural policy, is headed and staffed by a different party than the Finance Ministry. In addition, the recommended structural reforms consist of reducing subsidies and other measures to free up market forces. These are bound to be unpopular and difficult for a coalition government to implement. Thus, the German government has informally welcomed the potential for outside pressure that the coordination process offers, to strengthen the hand of domestic forces pressing for structural reform.

Japan's practice contrasts sharply with that of the others. Elected officials have repeatedly used *gaiatsu* to press for policy changes that domestic interest groups have resisted. Because of the strong preference in Japanese politics for harmonious international relations, *gaiatsu* has been an important factor in overcoming domestic resistance to change.

THE TURNOVER PROBLEM

In the 5½ years since the September 1985 Plaza Agreement there has been a large turnover in senior players involved in the G-7's deliberations, with a number of changes concentrated in the period between late 1988 and December 1989 (figure 3.1). Only three players present at the Plaza were still involved in 1990—David Mulford from the US Treasury and Karl Otto Pöhl and Robin Leigh-Pemberton from the German and UK central banks, respectively.[5] This rapid change in personalities suggests that consistent national

---

5. The record is much better in the two countries that were added to make up the G-7 in 1987: Canada's Finance Minister Michael Wilson, Bank of Canada Governor John Crow, and Italy's

policies and international institutional backup (presently provided informally by the IMF, as noted above) are likely to be essential in providing continuity to the coordination process. Those participants with the longest continuous tenure are bound to influence the process disproportionately, and incidentally they tend to come from the central banks (which also tend to have stronger permanent analytical capacities in their bureaucracies). Treasuries are likely to experience more frequent turnover at the ministerial level because of political pressures on governments, and among officials because of bureaucratic and political factors affecting the tenure and promotion of senior civil servants generally.

THE RESTRICTED ROLE OF THE IMF

IMF participation in the G-7 process has had its weaknesses, which were not of its own making. One weakness relates to the highly informal basis on which IMF representatives are invited to participate. They are expected to provide many of the functions of a secretariat, but they are given no authority to be one. A second is that their participation in the substantive issues is incomplete: they are relied upon to provide analytical support for surveillance of economic performance and macroeconomic policies, but they are excluded from discussions of foreign-exchange market issues. At the analytical level, their exclusion creates an artificial split that does not reflect the way in which economies or financial markets function. As an institutional issue, this exclusion is even more anomalous because of the IMF's obligation to engage in surveillance of its members' exchange rate policies.

CONCLUSION

This survey of major characteristics of national economic policies, philosophies, and institutions has illustrated some of the forces at play in the G-7 process. As the next chapter will show, the medium-term consensus that emerged in the early 1980s heightened the remaining national differences

---

central bank governor Carlo Ciampi, as well as the Italian G-7 deputy Mario Sarcinelli, all participated continuously from 1987 through 1990.

over the proper objectives of and the appropriate time frame for coordination (and some participants were more deeply convinced of the medium-term perspective than others). The analysis in this chapter has also illustrated how differences within governments were bound to affect both the diagnosis of international economic problems and the negotiation of their solution. All of these problems might be surmountable with strong and continuous leadership; yet a remarkable aspect of G-5 and G-7 leadership during this period was its discontinuity, owing to a high degree of turnover among the participants.

4 The Framework and the Process

The long history of governments' pursuit of cooperative arrangements, summarized in chapter 2, provides a context for the latest cooperative episode, which began with the meeting at the Plaza in September 1985. Several factors played a role in the process inaugurated there. One was the convergence, in the early 1980s, of the major industrial nations' philosophical approaches on a less activist role for governments in the economy. This convergence was reflected in their approach to a policy problem that developed in the early and mid-1980s that cried out to be dealt with cooperatively.

To promote recovery after the severe 1980–81 recession, the major industrial countries had adopted different macroeconomic policy mixes. The United States had pursued tight monetary policy but had implemented a fiscal expansion in 1982, while authorities in Germany and Japan, determined to reverse the buildup of large public-sector deficits in the 1970s, had pursued fiscal consolidation. The US economy had begun to expand rapidly, while tight monetary and fiscal policies abroad contributed to sluggish growth. The result of this constellation of national policies was threefold: persistent high real interest rates worldwide, lasting long after the beginning of the recovery; rapid appreciation of the US dollar during the 1980–85 period; and buildup of the US current account deficit in the 1980–87 period.

Another factor was the second Reagan administration's abandonment in 1985 of the unilateralist attitude to international economic issues adopted in the first Reagan term (see chapter 2). The key influences that brought about this change—shifting domestic pressures resulting from the strong dollar, the apparent peaking of the dollar in early 1985, mounting protectionist pressures in Congress, and the change of economic leadership in the administration—have been described by Putnam and Bayne (1987, 196–223), Funabashi (1989, 65–86), and Destler and Henning (1989, 17–47).

The Plaza Agreement has been widely seen as representing a change in the Reagan administration's exchange rate stance from one favoring floating rates to one of exchange rate management. Much more was attempted at the Plaza, however, since it was recognized that a realignment of economic

policies would also be required if exchange rate management was to succeed. This realignment could be encouraged by joint surveillance of macroeconomic policies along the lines the G-5 treasury ministers had been pursuing since the Versailles Summit, but in a more formalized way. The US Treasury was aiming for a regular surveillance process that could lead to commitments to policy change. The Germans and Japanese, on the other hand, were skeptical. They believed that a formal surveillance process would either be ignored, as surveillance activities in the European Monetary System were at that time, or be used to pressure them into automatic policy changes (in particular to increase their domestic demand) in the absence of changes in the United States' own policies.

Following the decision to create the G-7 at the 1986 Tokyo Summit, work began among the treasury deputies to formulate a new framework for policy coordination.[1] That framework and the process by which it was developed and applied are the subject of this chapter. Table 4.1 lists the major meetings and agreements of the G-7 in which the framework was developed and implemented.

The process the G-7 developed for themselves consists of regular meetings and other communications among the G-7 authorities. This process, including its close relationship to the annual economic summits, is described in the next section. As this process developed, surveillance and coordination of economic policies came to be carried out in several meetings throughout the year of treasury ministers and central bank governors, and in meetings of the G-7 treasury deputies (central bank deputies were not included).

An analytical framework for carrying out policy coordination is presented in the third section of this chapter. It is partly based on that developed by Working Party 3 (WP3) of the Organization for Economic Cooperation and Development (chapter 2). The WP3 framework, which provides as a basis for comparison with that actually employed by the G-7, has three sequential elements: surveillance, in which the member countries' economic performance is monitored and interpreted according to an objective analytical basis;

---

1. A comprehensive conceptual paper setting out such a framework was prepared by a group of Canadian officials in 1986 and distributed to the other treasuries in 1987 (Joint Department of Finance/Bank of Canada Study Group 1987). This paper reviewed the recent history of economic policy cooperation, the economics of saving-investment imbalances, and the conceptual and practical issues involved in using objective indicators in a medium-term cooperative framework.

T A B L E 4.1 Mileposts in economic policy coordination, 1985–89

Event	Date and Location	Significance
Plaza Agreement	22 September 1985, New York	G-5 treasuries and central banks agreed to coordinate foreign-exchange market intervention to accelerate decline of already weakened dollar.
Tokyo Economic Summit	6 May 1986, Tokyo	Adopted multilateral surveillance, delegated it to treasury ministers, and expanded coordination process to G-7.
G-7 ministerial	27 September 1986, Washington	First of what have become regular meetings of G-7 treasury ministers coinciding with semiannual meetings of IMF Interim Committee and World Bank Development Committee.
Louvre Accord	22 February 1987, Paris	Adopted package of policy commitments and exchange rate understandings among G-7 aimed at stabilizing dollar.
Venice Economic Summit	10 June 1987, Venice	Adopted performance indicators for G-7 multilateral surveillance.
"Black Monday"	19 October 1987	Crisis in financial markets.
G-7 "telephone accord"	22–23 December 1987	Policy commitments and exchange rate understandings were made public after US budget summit produced two-year plan for budget savings.
Toronto Economic Summit	21 June 1988, Toronto	Adopted commodity price indicator and introduced multilateral surveillance of structural reforms.
G-7 ministerial	September 1989, Washington	Signaled official view that strong dollar was not in line with medium-term fundamentals.

the development of policy guidelines and objectives against which to judge both performance and policies; and the development of mechanisms to identify, encourage, and implement remedial policy actions. The examination of the analytical framework is in turn divided into two parts—macroeconomic performance and exchange rates—because of the unique relationship (discussed below) that developed between the two as the surveillance mechanism developed.

The Process

THE ECONOMIC SUMMITS

A special relationship exists between the G-7 treasury ministers and the government leaders who participate in the annual economic summits. Because of the economic focus of these meetings, treasury ministers have traditionally been summit participants. Ministers' meetings between summits are kept informal and carried out by the member countries themselves—there is no permanent secretariat.

The surveillance procedures adopted at the Tokyo Summit in 1986 injected an element of political accountability into the process: the treasury ministers were requested to make an annual report to the leaders at the summit. At the Venice Summit in 1987, the host treasury minister, Giovanni Goria, presented an oral report prepared in consultation with his colleagues. Since then ministerial reporting has become progressively less formal; political oversight of the adjustment process by the summit leaders has not been pursued in any direct way. Instead, leaders have broadly delegated economic matters to the ministers. In the absence of an economic crisis, the summit agenda has turned to other, political issues (such as international drug trafficking and the environment in 1989, and the reintegration of Eastern Europe in the world order in 1990) and to the Uruguay Round of GATT negotiations.

G-7 MINISTERIAL MEETINGS

Ministerial meetings are at the apex of the coordination process. Their purpose is policy-oriented: to review the implications of short- and medium-term projections of international economic performance and to consider remedial policy actions. The meetings are attended by the seven treasury ministers and central bank governors, the treasury deputies, and the Managing Director of the IMF. Decisions are not necessarily confined to these meetings, however. Much is discussed and decisions are often made by telephone; this happened frequently in late 1987 after the worldwide stock market crash in mid-October.

Since there is no formal chair and no formally designated secretariat for the G-7, agendas for meetings are drawn up and all logistical arrangements made by the host country. Ministerial meetings are chaired by the minister of the host country. The same custom is followed at the deputies' meetings.

By 1989 the G-5 had become for most purposes the G-7, although G-7 ministerial meetings are still sometimes preceded by a separate brief meeting of the G-5 to discuss foreign-exchange market issues. The positions of, and issues among, the United States, Germany, and Japan largely determine the issues addressed and decisions made by the group, and these are discussed informally by telephone. Relationships among the three are conducted with considerable caution, however: Germany takes particular care to keep the other Europeans informed, and the United States to keep Canada informed.

These surveillance sessions traditionally begin with a presentation by the Managing Director of the IMF, to provide an objective overview of the issues and make recommendations for addressing those issues effectively. This report is then followed by a *tour de table*, beginning with the ministers and central bank governors from the G-3. The ministers do most of the talking; the discussion ranges over the domestic situations in the various countries, views of the international situation, and questions for other participants or for the Managing Director. At the end of the *tour de table*, the Managing Director departs.

The discussion then moves to foreign-exchange market developments, and thereafter to decisions on relevant communiqué language (if one is to be issued)—this format allows for debate and reconciliation of positions on the various issues. The draft communiqué is prepared by the host country, in consultation with deputies from the other countries, and referred to the ministers and governors in advance of the meeting so as to eliminate as many differences as possible before the ministerial itself.

Ministerial discussions have occurred three times a year: at a special "benchmark" surveillance session early in the calendar year (e.g., in February 1989 and early April 1990) and at two other sessions held in conjunction with the semiannual meetings of the Interim Committee of the IMF and the Development Committee of the World Bank. At these sessions actual performance is compared with that expected at the time of the benchmark session.

In 1987 the major policy focus was (as it had been since the 1985 Plaza Agreement) on foreign-exchange market developments, implementation of Louvre Accord policy commitments, and setting up the surveillance process. By 1988, the discussions centered on accounting for the unexpectedly strong growth that had materialized after the stock market collapse and addressing associated inflationary concerns. A generalized tightening of monetary policy was favored by the central banks, and was not resisted by the ministers, although the degree of concern about inflation varied in degree from country to country. Complacency about adjustment of external imbalances was also beginning to set in.[2] By 1989, issues such as international debt strategy and enlargement of the IMF quotas were beginning to move up the agenda.

Several factors characterized the ministerial meetings during the 1985–89 period. One was a lack of continuity due to the changes in personnel noted in the previous chapter. The group of ministers who attended the Plaza and Louvre meetings was an experienced one, and one that shared a common concern to improve world economic performance. By 1988 this group had accumulated considerable experience in working together. The ambience of the group could be expected to change with the arrival of several new players in 1988 and 1989. US Treasury Secretary James Baker was the first to depart, in early 1988, to join then–Vice President George Bush's presidential campaign. Nicholas F. Brady, Baker's successor, was initially disadvantaged by the uncertainties of the election campaign; it was not until 1989 that he was in a position to take hold of the process. In late 1988, Kiichi Miyazawa resigned as Japanese Finance Minister because of his involvement in the Recruit affair. He was replaced by Tatsuo Murayama for the duration of the Takeshita government, and then by Ryutaro Hashimoto in mid-1989. German Finance Minister Gerhard Stoltenberg was assigned the defense portfolio in mid-1989 and was succeeded by Theo Waigel.

The ministers from three of the other four governments contributed scarcely better to preserving continuity; indeed, in the 1988–89 period, the only treasury minister who did not change was Canada's Finance Minister

---

2. Gyohten (1988) discusses the coordination process in the 1985–88 period and characterizes the approach as passing through three phases, beginning with emphasis on exchange rate realignment at the time of the Plaza, moving to macroeconomic policy coordination in 1986 and 1987, and then shifting in 1988 to a focus on structural reforms.

Michael Wilson (see figure 3.1).

A second change in the ministerial meetings from 1985 to 1989 was in the use of English as a lingua franca. Language matters in international financial relations. All the participants in the original G-5 group could associate with one another in English. By 1989, however, the situation had changed considerably. At times in 1989, particularly around the Paris Summit, when treasury ministers from Japan and Germany were sometimes joined by their economic ministry colleagues, ministerial meetings were conducted with three or four interpreters in the room as well. Understandably, the informality and give-and-take of the proceedings declined somewhat.

Informality and confidentiality of the proceedings have been valued by the participants almost above all else. In no other forum is this group of senior officials free to talk so frankly with colleagues from other countries. Policy bargaining at times became quite intense, but the meetings have been unique occasions to gain a better feel for the problems and the aims of the other major economies. In general, the atmosphere at ministerials has tended to be lower-keyed than at meetings among deputies.

DEPUTIES' MEETINGS

The G-7 treasury deputies meet more frequently than the treasury ministers. Their meetings are usually planned to coincide with other regularly scheduled international meetings at which all the G-7 participants attend, such as the quarterly meetings of WP3 at the OECD and the deputies' meetings of the Group of Ten. They meet at other times as well, however, depending on the urgency of the issues in which their governments have common interests. These meetings are arranged on a confidential basis in order to avoid attracting press attention and to avoid giving offense to non–G-7 participants at the coinciding international events (although at times the "open secret" of a G-7 deputies' meeting and its effect on the timing of other meetings have been taken to great lengths). Since mid-1989, as the agenda of common issues has expanded, the deputies have increased the frequency of their meetings, so that the length and frequency of meetings surrounding the WP3 and G-10 conferences has become less of an issue.

Aside from their attempts to keep a low profile, which date back to the days of the G-5 when the meetings were kept secret, deputies' meetings are characterized by informality. The length and content of agendas are determined by the host-country chair, usually in telephone conversations with the deputies of the three largest countries and then with the others.

Since 1987 the Economic Counsellor of the IMF has been deeply involved with the deputies in discussions of macroeconomic surveillance. Like the Managing Director at the ministerial meetings, he leaves the room before foreign-exchange market developments are discussed. At each session, deputies review, with the IMF representative, the short-term (12- to 24-month) forecasts. In 1987 and 1988, medium-term projections (over a five-year period) were also prepared by the IMF and were reviewed with an eye to their implications for compatibility of national projections and for internal consistency within national projections. These projections fell into disuse by the end of 1988, when current account projections turned out to be wrong. (This episode is discussed later in this chapter.)

The tone of these discussions has varied from sometimes-intense bargaining to intensely frank exchanges of views and information on common concerns at other times. In the sessions that began in 1987, bargaining usually dealt with burden sharing in the adjustment process, as the United States sought to persuade Japan and Germany to speed up growth of their domestic demand. At these and other times, members of the other four countries played useful roles as buffers and honest brokers.

Foreign-exchange market developments are regularly reviewed at these meetings, with deputies of the three largest countries contributing their views, followed by the other participants. Because of the differences in deputies' jurisdictions over foreign-exchange intervention, these discussions provide unique opportunities for exchanges of view. However, underlying conceptual differences about the role of the exchange rate in the adjustment process (described in the next section), and the absence of central bank deputies who in some cases have direct jurisdiction (e.g., Germany), meant that discussions have tended to be long and decisions difficult to reach.

Prior to ministerial meetings, deputies summarize the policy issues into a short report for discussion by the ministers and governors. A communiqué for the ministerial meeting is drafted by the deputy whose country is hosting the ministerial meeting. Text covering contentious issues is negotiated by telephone and at a deputies' meeting shortly before the ministerial. In this way, controversial issues are isolated for special attention by the ministers and governors.

At times, such as in 1988 when emerging inflationary pressures provoked concerns about the need to anchor the system, deputies have used ad hoc groups of officials to address technical issues. The commodity price indicator, for example, was developed by such an ad hoc group working with IMF staff.

The Analytical Framework

Decisions by the G-7 ministers and governors are based on a process framework designed to systematize the discussion of the issues before them. To place G-7 practices in perspective, it is useful to apply the framework developed by Crockett (1989) based on the 1966 report of WP3 of the OECD (see chapter 2). Crockett (1989, 347–51) identified three main elements of this framework:

- Surveillance, using statistical (also called "objective") indicators in projections of the effects of economic policies and in measuring actual performance, to assist in assessing the emergence of internal or external disequilibria;
- Policy objectives and guidelines, to be developed in the light of existing knowledge about the linkages between goals and policies, against which the member countries' economic performance can be appraised and remedial changes recommended if necessary;
- Adoption of recommended policy changes.

SURVEILLANCE

Selection of Indicators

The first step in the framework is to develop indicators for measuring economic performance and to provide early warning of the emergence of unsustainable trends. Conceptually, G-7 indicators are economic variables for which the individual countries set targets or that they use as instruments to meet those targets.

Target indicators reflect domestic policy objectives such as growth of real incomes, low inflation, and full employment. The quantitative targets adopted for these objectives may then be compared against actual performance. In similar fashion, a set of instruments that countries use to achieve their targets, including open market operations, public-sector expenditures, and tax rates, controlled by monetary and fiscal authorities, may be quantified and monitored. Often targets will be pursued by focusing on intermediate variables that are not directly under the control of the authorities, but that are causally connected to variables that are. These include interest rates and exchange rates, nominal income, and growth of monetary aggregates. International objectives may refer to what in the domestic economy would be intermediate variables, such as reduction of current account balances, stabilization of exchange rates, or reduction of protectionist pressures.[3]

In practice, the indicators adopted by the G-7 at the 1986 Tokyo Summit (listed in table 4.2) include indicators of domestic performance, such as GNP (or GDP) growth, inflation, and unemployment; indicators of intermediate variables, such as the fiscal deficit (as a ratio to GNP or GDP), current account and trade balances, exchange rates, and monetary growth rates; and indicators of policy instruments, such as interest rates and reserves. The selection of these variables reflects a concern that the focus of surveillance discussions be broad enough to identify the underlying causes of imbalances, not just the imbalances themselves. Surveillance of foreign-exchange developments is carried on separately from that of these macroeconomic indicators in the G-7 (and is discussed below).

The composite indicators that were added in 1987 and 1988 (table 4.2) were mostly aggregations of national indicators prepared by IMF staff. The commodity price indicator had a life of its own: it was developed in 1988 in a cooperative effort among technical officials and IMF staff, in response to US interest in developing a nominal anchor or early warning signal of emerging systemic inflation pressures. Two commodity baskets—one including and one excluding oil (but both including gold)—were to be tracked to identify potential inflationary pressures originating from inside or outside the industrial countries.

---

3. Although the overall objectives of G-7 surveillance might be analyzed by reviewing the content of the communiqués, their content is too general, and lends itself better to analysis of policy commitments, as is done in table 5.1.

T A B L E   **4.2   Performance indicators for surveillance as adopted by the G-7 governments**

Approved at Tokyo Summit (1986)

GNP growth rates	Inflation rates
Interest rates	Unemployment rates
Fiscal deficit as percentage of GNP	Current account and trade balances
Monetary growth rates	Foreign-currency reserves
Exchange rates	

Adopted in Louvre Accord (1987)

Growth	Inflation
Budget performance	Current account and trade balances
Monetary conditions	Exchange rates

Further refinements in 1987–88

GNP or GDP growth	Composite indicators:
Domestic demand growth	Real GNP or GDP growth
Inflation	Industrial production
Fiscal balances	Consumer prices
Current account and trade balances	Commodity prices
Monetary conditions	Monetary growth
Exchange rates	Short-term interest rates
	Long-term interest rates
	Employment growth rates
	Unemployment rates

Sources: Official texts of the communiqués of the meetings.

Monitoring

Indicators are monitored by comparing their targeted paths, obtained from econometric projections, with actual performance. Tables 4.3 through 4.7 summarize and compare publicly available projections, prepared by national authorities and by the IMF and the OECD, of the set of indicators chosen by the G-7 for particular attention in surveillance. These indicators are GNP or GDP growth, domestic demand growth, inflation (as measured by the GNP

TABLE 4.3 Real GNP growth in the G–7 countries, projected and actual, 1984–89ᵃ (percentages per year)

Country	1984	1985	1986	1987	1988	1989
Canada						
Authorities	4.9	3.1	3.7	2.8	2.8	3.0
IMF	5.0	3.1	2.4	3.6	3.2	3.2
OECD	4.8	2.8	3.3	3.3	2.3	3.0
Actual	6.3	4.8	3.3	4.0	4.4	3.0
Japan						
Authorities	n.a.	4.6	4.0	3.5	3.8	4.0
IMF	3.9	4.1	4.0	2.9	3.4	4.2
OECD	3.5	5.0	4.5	3.0	2.0	4.5
Actual	5.1	4.9	2.5	4.6	5.7	4.9
United States						
Authorities	5.3	3.9	3.4	3.1	2.9	3.2
IMF	5.0	4.0	3.3	3.5	2.7	2.8
OECD	4.5	3.0	2.8	3.8	2.8	3.0
Actual	6.8	3.4	2.7	3.4	4.5	2.5
France						
Authorities	1.0	2.0	2.1	2.8	2.9	3.5
IMF	0.6	1.7	1.7	2.2	1.8	2.4
OECD	0.5	2.0	2.0	2.5	2.0	3.0
Actual	1.3	1.9	2.5	2.2	3.9	3.6
Germany						
Authorities	2.5	2.5	3.0	2.5	2.0	2.5
IMF	2.6	2.4	3.1	3.0	2.1	1.9
OECD	1.8	2.8	2.8	3.0	2.0	2.5
Actual	3.3	1.9	2.3	1.6	3.7	3.9
Italy						
Authorities	2.0	2.5	2.8	3.5	2.8	3.0
IMF	1.9	2.5	2.6	2.5	2.3	2.4
OECD	2.0	2.5	1.8	2.8	2.5	3.5
Actual	3.0	2.6	2.5	3.0	4.2	3.2
United Kingdom						
Authorities	3.0	3.5	3.0	2.5	4.5	2.5
IMF	2.6	2.4	2.2	2.5	2.3	2.5
OECD	2.3	3.0	2.5	2.3	2.3	3.0
Actual	2.1	3.7	3.6	4.7	4.6	2.2

n.a. = not available.

a. Projections reported are one-step-ahead.

Sources: IMF projections are from International Monetary Fund, World Economic Outlook, various issues; OECD projections and actual figures are from Organization for Economic Cooperation and Development, OECD Economic Outlook, various issues. Authorities' projections are from the following sources: Canada, Department of Finance, annual budgets; United States, Office of Management and Budget, Budget of the United States Government, fiscal years 1985–90; Japan, Economic Planning Agency, Economic Outlook and Basic Policy Stance of Economic Management, various issues; Germany, Economic Ministry, Annual Report of the Federal Government, various issues; France, Economics Ministry, Projet de Loi de Finances, various issues; Italy, Bank of Italy, Servizio Studi; United Kingdom, Chancellor of the Exchequer, Financial Statement and Budget Report, various issues.

T A B L E **4.4** **Real domestic demand growth in the G–7 countries, projected and actual, 1984–89[a]** (percentages per year)

Country	1984	1985	1986	1987	1988	1989
Canada						
Authorities	n.a.	2.9	3.7	2.9	2.4	3.1
IMF	5.9	3.1	3.1	2.2	3.4	4.0
OECD	5.0	2.5	2.5	2.3	2.3	3.3
Actual	4.7	5.3	4.2	5.2	5.0	4.1
Japan						
Authorities	n.a.	4.4	4.3	4.1	4.8	4.7
IMF	2.9	3.7	3.4	4.4	4.4	4.9
OECD	3.0	4.5	3.8	4.3	2.3	5.0
Actual	3.8	4.0	4.1	5.4	7.6	5.9
United States						
Authorities	n.a.	n.a.	n.a.	n.a.	n.a.	n.a.
IMF	5.8	4.1	3.6	3.3	2.0	2.7
OECD	5.0	3.8	3.0	3.5	2.0	2.5
Actual	8.7	3.8	3.3	3.0	3.3	1.9
France						
Authorities	n.a.	1.6	2.0	2.5	1.9	2.5
IMF	–0.5	0.9	1.7	2.7	2.2	2.4
OECD	0.0	1.5	1.8	2.8	2.3	3.3
Actual	0.4	2.5	4.5	3.3	4.0	3.1
Germany						
Authorities	2.0	2.0	3.8	3.8	2.8	2.5
IMF	2.2	1.4	2.8	3.7	3.1	2.0
OECD	1.5	1.8	2.0	4.3	2.8	2.0
Actual	2.0	0.8	3.5	2.9	3.7	2.7
Italy						
Authorities	0.9	2.4	2.4	4.2	3.5	3.5
IMF	2.2	3.1	2.9	3.7	2.6	2.9
OECD	2.3	2.5	1.8	3.3	3.3	4.0
Actual	3.9	2.7	2.9	4.7	4.7	3.3
United Kingdom						
Authorities	3.5	3.0	4.0	3.5	6.0	2.5
IMF	3.0	2.6	2.5	3.2	3.0	3.8
OECD	2.5	3.0	2.8	3.3	3.0	3.8
Actual	2.6	2.8	4.3	5.5	7.6	3.1

n.a. = not available.

a. Projections reported are one-step-ahead.

Sources: See table 4.3.

T A B L E   **4.5   Inflation in the G–7 countries, projected and actual, 1984–89[a]** (percentages per year)

Country	1984	1985	1986	1987	1988	1989
Canada						
Authorities	5.2	3.6	3.8	4.0	3.3	4.5
IMF	4.9	4.7	4.1	3.5	3.5	3.9
OECD	6.0	3.8	3.3	2.5	3.5	4.0
Actual	3.1	2.6	2.4	4.8	4.8	4.9
Japan						
Authorities	n.a.	2.8	1.9	1.6	1.3	2.0
IMF	n.a.	n.a.	2.1	0.5	1.6	1.6
OECD	1.5	2.8	1.5	0.0	1.8	1.0
Actual	2.3	2.0	0.6	0.1	0.7	2.3
United States						
Authorities	4.5	3.8	3.5	3.3	3.5	3.9
IMF	4.1	4.4	3.7	3.4	3.8	3.2
OECD	5.0	3.8	3.5	2.5	4.0	4.5
Actual	3.8	3.0	2.6	3.2	3.3	4.1
France						
Authorities	6.6	5.5	4.0	2.0	2.5	3.0
IMF	7.2	5.4	5.2	3.4	3.0	2.6
OECD	8.3	6.5	4.5	2.3	2.5	2.8
Actual	7.5	5.8	5.2	2.7	3.0	3.5
Germany						
Authorities	3.0	2.0	2.5	1.5	1.5	2.0
IMF	3.0	2.6	2.3	1.6	2.2	1.8
OECD	2.5	2.3	2.3	1.0	1.8	2.0
Actual	2.0	2.2	3.1	2.0	1.6	2.6
Italy						
Authorities	10.0	7.1	5.9	4.3	4.6	4.3
IMF	12.2	11.7	7.9	5.4	5.3	5.1
OECD	12.3	8.8	7.3	4.3	4.3	4.0
Actual	11.4	9.0	7.6	5.8	6.3	6.3
United Kingdom						
Authorities	5.0	5.0	3.8	4.3	6.3	5.5
IMF	5.0	5.0	4.2	3.7	4.8	5.2
OECD	6.0	4.5	4.8	3.5	5.3	6.3
Actual	4.6	5.6	3.5	5.0	6.5	6.9

n.a. = not available.

a. The measure used is the GDP or GNP deflator, except in the case of Japan, where the consumer price index is used. Projections reported are one-step-ahead.

Sources: See table 4.3.

T A B L E   4.6   Current account balances in the G–7 countries, projected and actual, 1984–89[a] (billions of US dollars)

Country	1984	1985	1986	1987	1988	1989
Canada						
Authorities	n.a.	n.a.	n.a.	−5.9	−7.9	−12.6
IMF	−1.5	0.3	−1.3	−2.9	−9.2	−11.9
OECD	3.5	0.3	2.5	−3.0	−4.0	−10.0
Actual	2.1	−1.5	−7.3	−6.9	−8.3	−14.1
Japan						
Authorites	n.a.	34.8	61.7	87.1	74.9	71.0
IMF	27.5	40.0	55.3	74.1	83.2	80.9
OECD	21.8	40.0	48.0	70.8	87.0	77.0
Actual	35.0	49.2	85.8	87.0	79.6	57.2
United States						
Authorities	n.a.	n.a.	n.a.	n.a.	n.a.	n.a.
IMF	−73.0	−115.0	−148.0	−123.0	−140.6	−128.7
OECD	−37.5	−130.5	−145.3	−124.8	−126.0	−116.0
Actual	−99.0	−122.3	−145.4	−162.3	−128.9	−110.0
France						
Authorities	n.a.	n.a.	n.a.	n.a.	n.a.	n.a.
IMF	0.0	0.2	2.1	6.5	−4.0	−2.8
OECD	−4.0	2.0	2.8	5.5	−1.0	−6.0
Actual	−0.8	−0.3	2.4	−4.4	−3.5	−3.9
Germany						
Authorities	15.1	19.2	34.1	55.1	59.2	67.0
IMF	4.0	5.8	15.7	25.5	32.5	41.5
OECD	2.0	7.5	18.5	21.8	29.0	51.0
Actual	9.9	16.5	39.7	45.8	50.4	55.4
Italy						
Authorities	0.4	−1.7	−6.5	5.2	−1.6	−5.1
IMF	0.5	−2.1	−7.9	3.0	−1.9	−4.2
OECD	−2.0	−1.8	−4.0	3.3	−1.0	−6.0
Actual	−2.5	−3.7	2.6	−1.5	−6.0	−10.5
United Kingdom						
Authorities	2.7	3.9	5.7	−4.1	−7.1	−23.8
IMF	2.0	1.5	1.8	−1.3	−3.5	−19.0
OECD	1.3	−0.3	1.8	−0.8	−6.0	−26.0
Actual	2.5	4.2	0.1	−6.0	−26.0	−31.3

n.a. = not available.

a. Authorities' projections are converted to US dollars using actual exchange rates where original data were in national-currency terms. Projections reported are one-step-ahead.

Sources: See table 4.3.

TABLE 4.7 Trade balances in the G–7 countries, projected and actual, 1984–89[a] (billions of US dollars)

Country	1984	1985	1986	1987	1988	1989
Canada						
Authorities	n.a.	n.a.	n.a.	n.a.	n.a.	n.a.
IMF	n.a.	n.a.	n.a.	n.a.	n.a.	n.a.
OECD	17.5	16.0	18.3	12.8	11.0	10.0
Actual	16.0	12.6	7.6	9.1	8.9	5.7
Japan						
Authorities	n.a.	44.9	67.6	91.3	84.3	88.0
IMF	n.a.	n.a.	n.a.	n.a.	n.a.	n.a.
OECD	35.3	48.5	56.0	80.8	133.8	99.0
Actual	44.3	56.0	92.8	96.5	95.0	77.1
United States						
Authorities	n.a.	n.a.	n.a.	n.a.	n.a.	n.a.
IMF	n.a.	n.a.	n.a.	n.a.	n.a.	n.a.
OECD	−61.8	−134.5	−136.8	−130.3	−139.8	−102.0
Actual	−122.2	−122.2	−144.5	−158.9	−126.7	−115.0
France						
Authorities	−0.8	0.2	0.7	−2.0	−5.4	−7.6
IMF	n.a.	n.a.	n.a.	n.a.	n.a.	n.a.
OECD	−4.8	−1.3	0.0	1.5	−7.3	−9.0
Actual	−4.7	−5.3	−2.1	−8.7	−8.1	−10.0
Germany						
Authorities	n.a.	n.a.	n.a.	n.a.	n.a.	n.a.
IMF	n.a.	n.a.	n.a.	n.a.	n.a.	n.a.
OECD	26.5	27.0	36.8	47.3	54.8	81.0
Actual	22.3	28.5	55.7	69.9	78.7	77.0
Italy						
Authorities	n.a.	n.a.	n.a.	n.a.	n.a.	−5.1
IMF	n.a.	n.a.	n.a.	n.a.	n.a.	n.a.
OECD	−4.8	−5.3	−8.5	0.3	−4.3	−5.0
Actual	−5.8	−6.1	4.5	0.0	−1.2	−12.0
United Kingdom						
Authorities	n.a.	−3.2	−7.3	−18.0	−20.5	−35.3
IMF	n.a.	n.a.	n.a.	n.a.	n.a.	n.a.
OECD	−1.0	−5.0	−4.5	−9.8	−17.5	−39.0
Actual	−6.1	−2.7	−12.8	−18.0	−37.0	−39.0

n.a. = not available.

a. Authorities' projections are converted to dollars using actual exchange rates where original data were in national-currency terms. Projections reported are one-step-ahead.

Sources: See table 4.3.

or GDP deflator), and current account and trade balances. Although the data submitted by national authorities are kept confidential, the publicly available data summarized in the tables illustrate the focus of the analytical discussions. They also show how the international agencies' estimates tended to lag turning points in some of the key indicators, and how in the early stages of the surveillance process few national authorities published projections of current account balances, which were a major policy focus. By 1989, however, the United States was the only one of the largest countries that did not; the budget for fiscal year 1990 contains a range estimate (Executive Office of the President 1990).

Both the OECD and the IMF use multicountry econometric models for policy analysis, as distinct from forecasting, to examine the channels by which spillovers can be transmitted among economies. Both models are widely used in assessing the overall world economic outlook for the medium term.[4] One of the values of these models is that base case simulations can be carried out, holding existing policy parameters such as exchange rates and oil prices constant, in order to examine the implications of the base case, and alternative simulations can be performed to gain insights into the consequences of changing the parameters.

National projections reflect the differing national economic frameworks and philosophies summarized in chapter 3, and have been sources of conceptual and measurement differences in the surveillance exercise. The methods used in most of the G-7 countries in making these projections resemble the base case methodology used by the IMF.

In the United States, the *Economic Report of the President,* prepared by the Council of Economic Advisers and released each January prior to transmission of the budget to Congress, provides a 12- to 18-month base case forecast, which is supplemented by projections that extend over a five-year period. These projections are prepared jointly by the Council of Economic Advisers, the Office of Management and Budget, and the Treasury. Whereas policy is assumed to remain unchanged in the short-term forecast, the five-year projections, based on certain stated economic and policy assumptions, resemble policy-endogenous targets. These assumptions are updated at the time of budget review in July. Similar forecasts are prepared

---

4. The IMF's model projections appear in its *World Economic Outlook,* and the OECD's in its *OECD Economic Outlook*; both are published semiannually.

independently by the Congressional Budget Office. The staff of the Federal Reserve prepares its own projections eight times a year, which are available to US officials; the Fed also publishes semiannual "central tendency" forecasts of the Federal Open Market Committee participants.

Canada prepares an annual short-term forecast that is published with the federal government's budget each February. At the same time a set of five-year base case projections is also made public. This economic and fiscal framework provides guidance for the 10 provincial government budgets that are introduced each spring.

In Germany, short-term forecasts and medium-term projections are made public with the annual budget. These are prepared jointly by the economics and finance ministries in consultation with the Bundesbank. In addition, five independent economic institutes prepare short-term forecasts, which are made public, as do the five "wisemen" on the Council of Economic Advisers. In France, the Ministry of the Economy, Finance, and Budget prepares a two-year forecast in the spring, which is updated in the autumn after budget negotiations have been completed and before the budget is adopted. UK budgets are two-stage affairs, and this affects the forecasting cycle; spending estimates are tabled in Parliament in the autumn along with an official outlook for the economy; revenue requirements are then tabled in the spring along with an economic update. Italian official forecasts are made available by the Bank of Italy; budgets are presented to Parliament by the Minister of the Treasury, usually in the autumn, after consultation with the Ministry of the Budget (the ministry responsible for planning and priorities) and the Treasury Ministry (responsible for revenues and tax collection).

Japan's projection methods differ the most from those of the international agencies, in that the Japanese national authorities set targets that reflect intended policy actions. As in the United States and Germany (but unlike in Canada and the other European countries, where forecasting and budgetary processes are more centralized in the treasuries), responsibility for preparation of projections is shared among agencies. The annual economic outlook, prepared by the Economic Planning Agency and the Ministry of Finance, emphasizes performance estimates for domestic demand and for trade and current account balances. Projections are released at the time of budget preparation in the spring and are approved by the Cabinet. These projections are for one fiscal year only and are actually a combination of target and projection; in other words, policy is endogenous to the projections. The numbers that are published incorporate the results of detailed industry studies as well as a consensus among officials of the feasible "policy effort" that can be expected in the coming year—to promote growth in domestic demand, to foster adjustment, and to restrain inflation, for example.

Differences in national practices were particularly noticeable when the G-7 inaugurated the macroeconomic surveillance process in mid-1987. An informal paper, authored at the US Treasury, proposed a procedure that resembled US (and IMF) procedures for formulating medium-term (five-year) objectives and projections for each of the participants. These projections were intended to provide the basis for an internal consistency check within the group as a whole, and in relation to the rest of the world economy. They would also provide a benchmark against which short-term performance of each economy, and the group as a whole, could be monitored in the course of each year.

IMF staff became involved in the process and organized the data collection and analysis. Most of the analytical work has been carried out by IMF staff in conjunction with regular Article IV consultations, although the policy analysis and recommendations are carried out for the G-7 by the Economic Counsellor on a highly confidential basis.

The initial exercise in the summer of 1987 revealed several differences in national practices. Measurements of certain variables reflected political and organizational differences among governments. Some countries' measures of fiscal balance, for example, were calculated as the balance of all levels of government (general government), whereas others focused on measures of the central-government balance. There were also differences in the techniques used for projections and the purposes to which they were put: some countries supplied policy-endogenous forecasts, whereas others supplied base case projections in which policies were assumed to remain unchanged.

Another area of difference was in governments' willingness to make projections available, even on a confidential basis, to other governments and the IMF. The United Kingdom, for example, was reluctant to submit unemployment data. Other countries, such as Germany, were reluctant to provide monetary or interest rate projections of any kind. Japan was reluctant to provide projections for five years out, arguing that the annual economic outlook reflected intended policies, which could not possibly be predicted more than a year in advance. The basis for the reluctance in each case was that these data might become public and undermine the authorities' policy flexibility. Initial resolution of some of these questions and differences required special visits to capitals by IMF staff to discuss and resolve the problems.

The initial effort was sufficiently successful that deputies were able to review an IMF synthesis of the data at their preparatory meeting in early September 1987. The aim of this discussion was to summarize trends in key indicators for the participant countries and for the group as a whole. This summary then formed the basis for discussion of policy options to be considered by ministers and governors at a meeting coinciding with the IMF-World Bank annual meetings in Washington. At this meeting, the role of the Managing Director of the IMF was also defined. It was similar to the role he had played with the G-5 following the 1982 summit: the Managing Director was to lay out his views, as an objective observer and representative of the interests of the rest of the world, of the economic outlook and policy priorities.

Since that time the surveillance process has become established in an annual cycle. The definition and measurement of the indicators were worked out in considerable detail at a marathon deputies' meeting, to which the IMF was invited, in January 1988. Early in each calendar year, governments were to submit a set of five-year projections for indicators of growth in output, domestic demand, inflation, fiscal balances, current account and trade balances, and monetary conditions. Where there were data problems such as those cited above, IMF staff were to resolve them, often using their own estimates, in consultation with the national authorities. These projections were to be analyzed and fleshed out by the IMF and presented alongside its own independent estimates.

Errors in Forecasting

Much of 1988 was relatively smooth sailing in the world economy—a surprise in the wake of the global stock market collapse of October 1987. Almost-universal predictions of recession were replaced by concerns about inflation and the possibility that central banks might not have withdrawn enough of the liquidity added in October and thereafter. These concerns were an important focus of WP3 discussions between treasury and central bank representatives, as well as those carried on in the G-7. In response to repeated reports of strong growth, central banks preemptively tightened monetary policy in the late spring and summer, and inflation seemed to stabilize in the OECD region around an average of 4 percent.

In addition, trade adjustment in the United States and Japan was faster and greater than projected by the IMF. As a result, the projections on which the surveillance exercise was based were called into question, making it difficult to agree on the implications for further policy change. The publicity resulting from the discrepancy increased pressure on ministers to take policy action they did not believe was required. Although one could dispute the actual numbers, the implication of the trend was correct: with no further policy change, and unchanged exchange rates, adjustment of current account imbalances could be expected to peter out. Only if structural changes favoring adjustment were occurring in the major countries, as some argued was the case, would current account balances continue to decline from their still-high levels—and such changes could not be measured *ex ante* in econometric models.

Surveillance of Foreign-Exchange Markets

Foreign-exchange market developments are reviewed regularly by deputies and discussed among the ministers and governors when changes in objectives or guidelines for the conduct of concerted intervention were under review. These developments are reviewed separately from macroeconomic performance. The measure of exchange rates has been nominal bilateral rates, which are the rates on which financial markets focus. More sophisticated measures, such as equilibrium exchange rates, are not used.

Analysis is informal, with views of participants exposed in a *tour de table*, beginning with the three large countries. In general, discussion focuses on possible reasons for recent developments and then moves to a review of whether change in existing confidential understandings regarding concerted intervention is required. If recent exchange market developments are unexpected, informal telephone discussions between the United States and Japan, and the United States and Germany, have preceded the meeting.

Although the views of the participants from these three countries are major factors in the discussion, the views of others are important as well. The French, for example, have tended to stress the importance they attached to preserving the credibility of reference ranges; participants from some other countries have placed more emphasis on fundamentals. These views, however, tended to come out in protracted discussions of the mechanics of intervention rather than in discussion directed at the nature of the coordination regime itself.

Yet these differing views did have a profound and direct impact on how coordination was developed after the Tokyo Summit. A classic illustration is the difference between the substance and the interpretation of the February 1987 Louvre Accord. Consider the economic environment at that time. US employment levels were high and domestic demand was robust, but the fiscal deficit was approximately 5 percent of GNP, and the current account deficit was close to $140 billion, despite the substantial depreciation of the dollar that had taken place in the previous two years. One might have been tempted to say that the solution would come with time, as the economy adjusted to the new relative prices brought about by the dollar's decline. However, the effects of changes in relative prices were appearing very slowly. It was also clear that capacity constraints in the US economy soon would begin to bind, and that this would reinforce the eventual inflationary impact of the dollar's decline.

The Japanese and German economies mirrored that of the United States. Both were running large current account surpluses, and growth was still sluggish. Unemployment in Europe was uncomfortably high, but the consensus was that this reflected a high natural rate of unemployment, due to restrictive regulations and other distortions, more than it did a lack of stimulus to aggregate demand.

Throughout this period, the differential between US interest rates and those in Germany and Japan narrowed, thereby reducing the relative attractiveness of dollar-denominated assets, despite the coordinated round of discount rate cuts in the spring of 1986 and market perceptions that US monetary policy would have to tighten that year. By December 1986 the nominal value of the deutsche mark had climbed to 2.02 from 3.31 to the dollar in March 1985, a 64 percent revaluation; in Japan, the yen had climbed to ¥162.29 from ¥260.24 at the dollar's peak in February 1985, a 60 percent nominal revaluation.

Policies appropriate to deal with these problems would have included a reduction of the US fiscal deficit to restrain growth in domestic demand (fiscal tightening would also have been appropriate in Canada and Italy, two other countries with large fiscal deficits). To maintain world demand while US demand was being restrained, stimulation of demand in countries with excess capacity would have been helpful. Countries with structural rigidities, especially in Europe, should have undertaken microeconomic reforms to remove obstacles to growth and adjustment. Finally, some further depreciation of the US dollar might have been necessary.

This was essentially the policy package adopted at the Louvre meeting. An objective stated in the communiqué from the meeting was "the reduction of large unsustainable trade imbalances . . . [as] a matter of high priority," and the accord committed the G-7 governments to policy measures to help achieve those objectives. Exchange rates were to be " . . . broadly consistent with underlying fundamentals, *given the policy commitments summarized in this statement* [emphasis added]."

Yet the main focus during both the preparation for the Louvre meeting and at the meeting itself was on the mechanics of exchange market intervention.[5] And since the meeting the widespread public perception has been that the Louvre Accord was first and foremost a currency agreement.

Why this focus on exchange rates instead of on policy adjustment? The answer is that governments were engaged in regime preservation.[6] By mid-1986 Japan and Germany were increasingly worried that further appreciation of their currencies would put an excessive burden on their exporters and lead to recession and rising unemployment. US Treasury Secretary Baker, mindful of the approaching 1988 presidential election, was interested in sharing the burden of adjustment and saw an opportunity for a bargain: in exchange for US cooperation to stabilize currency relationships (US officials had been engaged in "talking down the dollar" up to this point), Japan and Germany might be persuaded to stimulate domestic demand. Other countries were pushing at the same time for a surveillance process that would get at the underlying problem of domestic imbalances and avoid an exclusive focus on exchange rates, which they saw as only a symptom of that problem.

The persuasive argument for stabilizing the dollar was that a pause in exchange rate realignment was needed, both to allow adjustments that had occurred to date to feed through the system and to prevent undesirable overshooting. But beyond that the United States was forced by developments in early 1987 to bring an end to the dollar's decline. Rising domestic inflationary concerns and dependence on continued capital inflows to finance the twin deficits—fiscal and current account—contributed to a compelling need to stabilize the dollar before a Treasury bond auction in February. These factors persuaded Baker to enter into the currency stabilization ar-

---

5. Funabashi's account of the meeting (1989, chapter 8) also reflects this focus.

6. Kenen (1988, 5) describes what he calls the "regime preserving" approach to policy coordination as follows: "Mutual persuasion takes the place of adversarial bargaining; exchange rate stabilization becomes a public good rather than a rule for optimizing policies."

rangements at the Louvre.

The difference between the substance of the Louvre Accord (i.e., policy changes) and the focus at the ministerial meeting that produced the accord (i.e., exchange market intervention) was also a symptom of differing views of the surveillance process that was being developed at the time. One view, held by France and Italy, and from time to time by the US Treasury, reflected an approach to coordination based on exchange rate intervention: if there were pressure on key exchange rates, the presumption was that coordinated intervention should be used and/or macroeconomic policies should be changed. The practical problem was that this view implied that the *only* channel of adjustment could be policy change: only if it could be demonstrated that changing policies would not correct the problem would exchange rates be changed.

The other view, held by Japan, Germany, the United Kingdom, and Canada—and sometimes by the US Treasury—was that the central objective was to reduce external imbalances. Adjusting fiscal policies would remove the underlying shock that gave rise to the misalignment of exchange rates and the current account imbalances, but the response to that adjustment would necessarily include a realignment of real exchange rates. Monetary policy could act to hold nominal exchange rates fixed though this transition, but this would put the entire burden of adjustment on domestic price levels. In this view, then, exchange rates were an instrument of adjustment.

Conceptually, the starting points of these two approaches differ. The presumption in the first view is that if there is pressure on exchange rates, something should be done (intervene or change policies), if anything can be done, to keep the exchange rate unchanged. The presumption of the second approach is that if there is pressure on the exchange rate, it reflects changes in the "fundamentals"; changes in exchange rates may well be required to keep them in line with these fundamentals.

The endpoint of the two approaches, however, should be the same: agreement to one or more of intervention or changes in monetary or fiscal policies. In practice, however, disagreements arose about what was "fundamental," that is, requiring changes in exchange rates, and about whether intervention would also require changes in short-term interest rate policy (especially if such changes would conflict with the domestic objectives of monetary policy). These differences of view continue to have an important effect on the evolution of the coordination process.

POLICY OBJECTIVES AND GUIDELINES

The second element in a successful coordination framework, according to Crockett (1989), is a set of policy guidelines, which are developed to guide surveillance of members' policies and performance and to identify the need for remedial action. G-7 practice has been to make policy commitments and exchange rate objectives public in communiqués issued at ministerial meetings. In this section, exchange rate commitments are analyzed first, together with the measures that were used for comparing commitments with actual performance; the norms that were used in judging the need for changes in macroeconomic policies are then analyzed.

Exchange Rate Objectives

The decisions at the 1985 Plaza meeting and the 1987 Louvre meeting to undertake coordinated intervention in foreign-exchange markets were made against a historical background of intergovernmental debate. Governments' public commitments on exchange rates during the 1985–89 period and their views on appropriate levels, as expressed in G-7 communiqués, are summarized in table 4.8. These commitments illustrate the change in objectives from realignment of key currency relationships in 1985 to stabilization in 1987. Behind these publicly stated objectives, however, lay the disagreement, outlined above, about the role of the exchange rate in the adjustment process and ambivalence about exchange rate management.

Ironically, during this same period exchange rates were being managed increasingly successfully by the four G-7 members of the European Monetary System (EMS). When it was created in 1979, the main purposes of the EMS were to promote convergence in economic performance among participating countries and to promote a zone of monetary stability in Europe that might withstand global instability. EMS exchange rates are fixed but adjustable. The exchange rate mechanism (ERM) provides publicly stated rules for marginal intervention (which is compulsory when a currency diverges by more than a fixed amount from its central rate, expressed as the value of the ecu in the country's currency).

Exchange rates in the EMS are to move only in response to inflation differentials (although those who believe in the need for convergence in inflation rates in the EMS countries argue that even this movement should be restricted in order to promote convergence in economic performance) and in

TABLE 4.8 Exchange rate objectives agreed to by the G-5 and G-7, 1985–90

Event	Communiqué language
Plaza Agreement, 22 September 1985, New York	" ... agreed that exchange rates should play a role in adjusting external imbalances ... exchange rates should better reflect fundamental economic conditions than has been the case ... in view of the present and prospective changes in fundamentals, some further orderly appreciation of the main non-dollar currencies against the dollar is desirable. ..."
Tokyo Summit, 6 May 1986	" ... remedial efforts focus first and foremost on underlying policy fundamentals ... intervene in exchange markets when to do so would be helpful."
G-7 treasury ministers' meeting, 27 September 1986, Washington	Agreed that "cooperative efforts need to be intensified" to reduce external imbalances " ... without further significant exchange rate adjustment."
Louvre Accord, 22 February 1987, Paris	"The Ministers and Governors agreed that the substantial exchange rate changes since the Plaza Agreement will increasingly contribute to reducing external imbalances and have now brought their currencies within ranges broadly consistent with underlying economic fundamentals, given the policy commitments summarized in this statement. Further substantial exchange rate shifts among their currencies could damage growth and adjustment prospects in their countries. In current circumstances, therefore, they agreed to cooperate closely to foster stability of exchange rates around current levels."

Event	Communiqué language
G-7 treasury ministers' meeting, 8 April 1987, Washington	" . . . reaffirmed the view that around current levels their currencies are within ranges broadly consistent with economic fundamentals . . . and the basic policy intentions outlined at the Louvre meeting."
Venice Summit, 10 June 1987	" . . . Given the policy agreements reached at the Louvre and in Washington, further substantial shifts in exchange rates could prove counterproductive to efforts to increase growth and facilitate adjustment."
G-7 treasury ministers' meeting, 26 September 1987, Washington	" . . . reaffirmed that currencies are within ranges broadly consistent with . . . fundamentals."
G-7 communiqué, 22–23 December 1987	" . . . agreed that either excessive fluctuation of exchange rates, a further decline of the dollar, or a rise in the dollar to an extent that becomes destabilizing to the adjustment process, could be counterproductive by damaging growth prospects in the world economy. They reemphasized their common interest in more stable exchange rates among their currencies and agreed to continue to cooperate closely in monitoring and implementing policies to strengthen underlying economic fundamentals to foster stability of exchange rates."
Toronto Summit, 21 June 1988	"We endorse the Group of Seven's conclusion that either excessive fluctuation of exchange rates, a further decline of the dollar, or a rise in the dollar to an extent that becomes destabilizing to the adjustment process, could be counterproductive by damaging growth prospects in the world economy."

Table continues next page

Event	Communiqué language
G-7 treasury ministers' meeting, 24 September 1988, Berlin	" . . . emphasized their continued interest in stable exchange rates among their currencies. . . reaffirmed their commitments to pursue policies that will maintain exchange rate stability. . . ."
G-7 treasury ministers' meeting, 2 April 1989, Washington	"The exchange rate stability over the past year has made a welcomed contribution to, and has been supported by, the progress achieved in sustaining the global expansion and reducing external imbalances. . . . agreed that a rise of the dollar which undermined adjustment efforts, or an excessive decline, would be counterproductive. . . ."
Sommet de l'Arche, 17 July 1989, Paris	No reference to exchange rates
G-7 treasury ministers' meeting, 23 September 1989, Washington	" . . . considered the rise in recent months of the dollar inconsistent with longer run economic funda-mentals. . . . agreed that a rise of the dollar above current levels or an excessive decline could adversely affect prospects for the world economy."
G-7 treasury ministers' meeting, 7 April 1990, Paris	" . . . expressed the need . . . for greater stability in exchange markets . . . discussed developments in global financial markets, especially the decline of the yen against other currencies, and its undesirable consequences for the global adjustment process, and agreed to keep these developments under review."
Houston Summit, 11 July 1990	No reference to exchange rates
G-7 treasury ministers' meeting, 22 September 1990, Washington	" . . . exchange rates were now broadly in line with continued adjustment of external imbalances."

Sources: Official texts of the communiqués of the meetings.

response to secular changes in supply, demand, or relative prices. To abide by these rules, members must also be prepared to change monetary policy at short notice, which means sacrificing domestic policy independence. The anchor for price levels in the system has been provided by Germany, whose monetary policy has consistently been conducted so as to maintain low inflation.

In their blueprint for an international monetary regime, Williamson and Miller (1987) proposed a more flexible system of target zones, in which exchange rate misalignments would be measured by deviations of the real effective exchange rate from an agreed fundamental equilibrium exchange rate (FEER) estimate.[7] Adjustment of the target zones would occur as follows:

> For operational purposes one has to translate a target for the *real* exchange rate into one for the *nominal* exchange rate. The implication of having a target specified in real terms is that as new statistics on differential inflation become available one would automatically make whatever adjustments in the nominal targets were needed to keep the real targets unchanged. Since data on price movements are published monthly, individual changes in the nominal target zones will be modest. Thus, nominal zones would crawl over time to maintain the real zones constant. (Williamson and Miller 1987, 11)

The use from time to time of reference ranges in G-7 exchange rate management[8] differed from EMS practice and blueprint concept. Exchange rates are expressed in nominal bilateral terms in the G-7, and ranges have been kept confidential (a practice that is respected in this study). Fixing the nominal rate in a world of differing inflation rates creates distorted signals for international trade. Real exchange rates are a superior measure because they reflect differential rates of inflation, which affect import and export decisions. A more convenient measure of medium-term equilibrium relationships than bilateral real exchange rates for each pair of currencies is the real *effective* exchange rate index, which measures trends in the real (i.e., infla-

---

7. The FEER is defined as the rate "which is expected to generate a current account surplus or deficit equal to the underlying capital flow over the cycle, given that the country is pursuing 'internal balance' as best it can and not restricting trade for balance of payments reasons" (Williamson and Miller 1987, 10).

8. Although the use of reference ranges by the G-7 has never been publicly acknowledged, Funabashi (1989) has reported in detail on this subject.

tion-adjusted) value of a currency relative to a basket of currencies of its major trading partners.

Underlying differences of view clouded questions of setting and changing exchange rate reference ranges. Proponents of ranges emphasized markets' need for publicly stated reference points for medium-term exchange rate expectations and argued that commitment by governments to exchange rate stability would provide greater discipline to macroeconomic policies.

Other influential arguments, however, recalled the views of the critics of fixed exchange rates.[9] These included the desire for confidentiality in order to preserve the element of surprise in intervention; the view that the exchange rate was only the messenger, signaling difficulties with prevailing macroeconomic policies; concern that manipulation of exchange rates to maintain reference ranges would be used as a substitute for policy changes; and the view that governments were not prepared to adjust domestic policies to satisfy exchange rate objectives.

The empirical literature on the costs and benefits of fixed and floating exchange rate systems also supported a skeptical stance. A recent survey of the empirical literature concluded as follows:

> Since clear agreement exists that real exchange rate variability increases with nominal exchange rate flexibility, the issue of the effects that such real exchange rate volatility may have becomes important; if such volatility of real exchange rates has clearly harmful effects, then fixed exchange rates become more attractive. It cannot be said, however, that any widely acknowledged effects of greater real exchange rate volatility have been found. With regard to the contention that greater exchange risk harms international investors and depresses the volume of international trade, the evidence does not support any conclusions against flexible exchange rates. The evidence suggests in fact that international investors may actually prefer the distribution of returns under floating exchange rates to that realized under fixed rates. The evidence on the effects of greater exchange risk on trade is mixed and at best leans slightly in the direction of suggesting that exchange rate volatility reduces the level of trade. In any case, the evidence on exchange rate volatility cannot be used to argue the case for fixed exchange rates. (Edison and Melvin 1990, 42)[10]

---

9. Frenkel and Goldstein (1986) evaluate the arguments on both sides of the debate.

10. Edison and Melvin also review the evidence on misalignment and find it insufficient to use for policy conclusions. They note: "The pessimistic conclusion from our consideration of the current state of knowledge on the determinants and implications of the choice of an exchange rate system is that any discussion of the proper role for policy must be based on conviction

These differences and the practice of secrecy ultimately contributed to erosion of the system's credibility. Secrecy was preferred to preserve the element of surprise in concerted intervention and to avoid market speculation. One of its unintended consequences, however, was to create the damaging impression that reference ranges were permanent; such an impression was created after the 1987 Louvre Accord and reinforced by references in subsequent communiqués and public statements to exchange rate stability and "current levels."

Involvement of the G-5 and G-7 in exchange rate management happened by experiment rather than by grand design. Before the 1985 Plaza meeting, some participants were skeptical that concerted intervention could push the dollar down sufficiently to dampen protectionist sentiments in the US Congress.[11] Nevertheless, concerted intervention was decided upon, and the operation succeeded beyond expectations.

Similarly, the slightly expanded group of participants at the Louvre meeting in 1987 included both skeptics and enthusiasts. All were willing to participate, at least on a temporary basis, in currency stabilization operations, but some had been pushing for broader economic surveillance. When again concerted intervention was seen to be effective in stabilizing key currency relationships, some participants interpreted the accord as a formal initiative designed to stabilize exchange rates—a kind of successor, but not a return, to Bretton Woods. The result was a managed float, but changes were not always managed in an orderly way.

UK Chancellor Nigel Lawson, speaking at the IMF–World Bank Annual Meetings in September 1987, stated his view of the advantages of managed floating:

> I believe that we can and should use the experience we have gained to build a more permanent regime of managed floating. I do not see the past two years simply as a temporary phase. Our objectives should be clear: to maintain the maximum stability of key exchange rates, and to manage any changes that may

---

rather than on fact" (Edison and Melvin 1990, 43).

11. Concerted intervention agreed upon at a G-5 meeting in January 1985 was followed by heavy intervention by the German authorities in February and March of that year, and " . . . by virtue of timing appears a likely candidate for the instrument that pricked the [speculative exchange rate] bubble" (Frankel, forthcoming, 1991b).

be necessary in an orderly way.[12]

The conduct and results of exchange market intervention are examined in the next chapter. One issue relating to exchange rate objectives that was left ambiguous was how to change reference ranges. Funabashi (1989) has described one instance after the Louvre meeting, in April 1987, when the yen was rebased against the dollar by the participants agreeing to set the range around the level reached in the markets at the close of the previous day. This was a reactive rather than proactive approach, but it was a compromise that the participants preferred because they could not agree on a common view of what the level should be and were skeptical of more formal estimates such as the equilibrium exchange rate.

Ranges were broadened in late 1987 when the dollar dropped, and again in 1989 when it strengthened, to the point where they had become devoid of much meaning. However, one very positive result of this development was that discussions of exchange market intervention became less mechanistic as time passed, and more judgmental and integrated with views of economic fundamentals.

Integrating Exchange Rates and Macroeconomic Surveillance

Adoption of multiple-indicator surveillance at the Tokyo Summit implied integrating the surveillance of exchange rates and of macroeconomic performance. Any understanding of the reasons for nominal and real exchange rate variability would be incomplete unless it were linked to an understanding of the reasons for changes in real as well as financial variables. Yet exchange rates and macroeconomic policies were set on two tracks in the G-7.

By 1989, when reference ranges had been broadened nearly to the point of meaninglessness, this segmentation began to break down. Discussions about concerted intervention became less mechanistic and more closely linked with underlying economic fundamentals.

The decision to set exchange rate and macroeconomic surveillance on two tracks was understandable, if not in the end well advised. One reason for the decision was that macroeconomic performance responded slowly to policy

---

12. Statement at the Joint Annual Discussion, Board of Governors of the International Monetary Fund, 1987 Annual Meeting, Washington, 30 September 1987.

stimulus (and the policy changes were themselves slow to bring about) compared with the speed with which things happened in exchange markets, and so more attention was paid to foreign-exchange market intervention; intervention policy also provided a ready means to be seen to be coordinating in a tangible way. Second, discussion of exchange rates tended to focus on the mechanistic issues of concerted intervention—particularly on attempts to establish rules for intervention and on the term, manner, and amount of intervention. Third, the differing weights and views among the various participants about the use and impact of concerted intervention meant that frequent discussion was required to interpret and respond to foreign-exchange market developments. Fourth, their own mandates covered foreign-exchange market intervention more clearly than they did macroeconomic policy.

A rules-based approach to coordination, favored by some of the G-7 participants, would have movements in key currencies (in relation to reference ranges) lead in an automatic way to consultation and concerted intervention. The more pragmatic approach favored by others relied on assessment of market sentiment and conditions as an essential part of analysis of exchange rate movements. These participants felt, sometimes strongly, that sterilized intervention was mainly a signaling device. Heavy persistent intervention, to be credible, should signal governments' intention to change policy (monetary policy being the easiest and quickest to change), or it should lead to reevaluation of the existing exchange rate objective.

A key weakness of the regime was that the approach to exchange rates was never conceptually coherent or related to some measure of equilibrium exchange rates. It also lacked direct central bank input in the preparatory stages of decision making (although matters were discussed informally between central bank and treasury officials in most national capitals), with the result that some central banks did not feel obliged to accept institutional responsibility for the decisions made—a major difference from the EMS. Another weakness was that concerted intervention, as time went by, was agreed upon only when it was pretty obvious that exchange rates had overshot. By implication, credibility was eroded as it became apparent that markets, more than governments, were determining reference ranges.

Guidelines for Macroeconomic Policies

Once emerging trends in economic performance have been identified and interpreted, agreement on remedial policy action, if required, is more likely to be reached when governments agree on how policies affect goals. Disagreements have arisen about linkages among economies, such as the dispute between the US and the German governments in the 1980s over the appropriate stance of fiscal policy. A leading scholar on these issues, Ralph C. Bryant, has summarized the problem as follows:

> There is great uncertainty about how policy actions and nonpolicy shocks originating in one nation influence economic developments in others. . . . Even when analysts agree about the sign of effects, moreover, little consensus exists about their empirical magnitude. . . . Individual governments do not even have at their disposal an agreed analytical framework for evaluating the effects of external forces on their domestic economies. . . . Insufficient public awareness of the extent of economic interdependence, which in turn contributes to a lack of political will by government officials, is also an important obstacle [to convergence in analytical views]. (Bryant 1987, 9–10)

One of the most comprehensive analytical efforts in this area is reported by Bryant et al. (1988), who took stock of 12 existing macroeconometric models and involved them in early 1986 in comparative simulations to study the similarities and differences in model results. Participants prepared simulations of changes in monetary and fiscal policy in the United States and non–US OECD countries. As Bryant has reported, there was broad agreement that the domestic impacts of policies were significant: the simulations generally agreed on the sign of the impact, but less frequently on magnitudes. With respect to external impacts, the models generally agreed that fiscal policies have significant effects (with even less agreement on magnitudes, however) and that monetary policies do not have significant external effects (and the direction of the effects is ambiguous).

Despite these efforts, most senior treasury officials have made little use of the results when they were brought to their attention, and they remain skeptical of the value and relevance of quantitative research to the problem at hand, preferring to rely on firsthand experience and back-of-the-envelope judgments about linkages.

This preference for informality extended to the adoption of policy guidelines as well. No agreed-upon principles on which to base judgments about policy changes, such as those in the Williamson-Miller blueprint, have been adopted in the G-7 process. Policy commitments have been made (and are summarized in table 5.1), but many were very general. Fiscal policies were an exception: the United States, Japan, Germany, and France were prepared to be quite specific about their commitments to fiscal change.

One suggestion for developing firmer guidelines was to develop clearly defined monitoring ranges around the indicators; breaching the ranges would then lead to discussion of policies to bring performance more into line with intentions.[13] Although this approach would have provided an objective set of criteria, it was dismissed with little discussion because of its implied automaticity.

Instead, the IMF was requested in 1989 to expand its projection exercise on an experimental basis to include scenarios in which the base case parameters were assumed to change. This approach, it was hoped, would provide a basis for discussions of options to bring actual performance more into line with intended performance in the medium term. Such scenarios were first published in the April 1989 *World Economic Outlook*; the alternatives chosen for simulation incorporated policy adjustments consistent with the goal of reducing imbalances to sustainable levels. One scenario assumed that the United States would achieve the Gramm-Rudman-Hollings deficit reduction targets. A second assumed that structural changes would be undertaken in other G-7 countries.

The result of these scenarios illustrated that if the policy changes occurred, a sustained improvement of the US current account deficit could be accomplished, together with a change in the pattern of growth in output and domestic demand, and lower inflation and interest rates than if no changes were made by the authorities (International Monetary Fund 1989, 31–38). Bergsten (1988, 82–83) used a similar approach, but went further: he recommended that the US administration set targets for eliminating the twin deficits and apply peer pressure on its trading partners for complementary action.

PEER PRESSURE AND CHANGES IN POLICIES

The third element of successful coordination in the Crockett (1989) framework is to find means to encourage remedial policy action once the need for it has been identified. In theory this can involve either peer pressure from other countries, bargaining to accomplish linkage with other desired objec-

---

13. The suggestion was made by US Treasury Secretary Baker in a speech to the International Monetary Conference in Chicago, 6 June 1988.

tives, or retaliation for failure to take the remedial action.

An early example of the use of peer pressure comes from the heyday of WP3 coordination: the chairman of that group would at times write to the authorities of an offending country to point out shortcomings and recommend desirable policy.[14] In the G-7, peer pressure was used in two cases in the late 1980s, with mixed success. Linkage was employed in some instances, such as in the bargaining between the United States and Japan in late 1986 and in the runup to the Louvre meeting, but not in others. The basis for peer pressure might have been targets for performance, such as Bergsten suggested, or some other norms. In practice the norms applied were based on the concept of changing patterns of growth in the largest countries in directions that would reduce external imbalances.

In the first example of the use of peer pressure, in 1986 and early 1987, the United States pressured Japan to stimulate domestic demand by expanding fiscal policy (this episode is examined in the next chapter). In the second case, in 1987 and 1988, the United States pressured Germany to use macroeconomic policies to stimulate domestic demand. While accepting the case for sharing the adjustment burden, the German government argued, and some others tended to agree, that structural rigidities in the German economy implied that the focus of stimulus should be on the supply side, not the demand side. (This disagreement illustrates one of the analytical differences in the coordination exercise over the effect of expansionary measures—the outcome came down to a matter of judgment by the German government.) The Germans further argued that stronger growth in domestic demand would be forthcoming without further stimulus (see table 4.4); however, when the expansion did appear it was mainly in output rather than domestic demand, with the result that the German current account surplus continued to climb. Another German argument was that most of its surplus was with Europe, not the United States, and therefore that excessive attention to its reduction would not solve the US deficit problem.

In a third episode, both peer pressure and linkage might have been used, but neither was (this is the case of "the dog that did not bark"). The issue was whether the incoming Bush administration in early 1989 could be persuaded by the non–US G-7 participants to administer further budget restraint. A key US priority at that time was that of reformulating the industrialized

---

14. This practice was made known to me by Stephen Marris.

countries' strategy for dealing with the external debt of middle-income Third World debtors. The G-7 could have linked concessions on this objective to demands for more US budget restraint, but neither such linkage nor much peer pressure was applied. One reason was the reluctance of the other participants to use linkage in this case. The new US debt strategy proposals, which would allow debtors implementing economic adjustments to use funds from the World Bank and the IMF and from the Japanese government to reduce their debt overhangs, was broadly in line with the thinking of others, but had hitherto been blocked by US insistence on the existing approach to the debt problem. Everyone wanted to get on with establishing a new framework as quickly as possible.

A second reason was that all of the participants had allowed the debt issue to crowd other items off the agenda, including macroeconomic surveillance. Complacency was growing about external imbalances, and anxiety about the prospects for financing them was declining.

The third reason was the most important. The new US administration had taken the initiative to identify the need for fiscal change and to assure its partners both of its good intentions and of the rosy prospects for reaching a bipartisan accord to eliminate the need for sequestration under the Gramm-Rudman-Hollings law. This fed the growing complacency with regard to external imbalances.

Improving the Functioning of the International Monetary System

From time to time, the G-7 participants looked beyond their informal and admittedly ad hoc surveillance arrangements to consider how to improve the functioning of the international monetary system. Early in 1988 Minister of Finance Edouard Balladur (1988) of France proposed consideration of three possible approaches to monetary reform: international cooperation, a "world EMS," and a monetary standard "that would play the role of [a] main world reserve asset." Although he did not advocate a particular choice, Balladur urged governments to consider systemic reform, arguing that floating exchange rates have been "one of the essential causes of the economic disorders of the past 15 years."

These alternatives were discussed by ministers and governors at the spring 1988 ministerial meeting and led to a decision that deputies of both the treasuries and the central banks should carry out a joint study of possible improvements. US views on the issue were made public in comments by Treasury Secretary Baker:

> What form and direction should this [monetary reform] take? It is tempting to consider sweeping, revolutionary changes in the system—particularly the exchange rate part of the system. But it is far from clear that such changes are desirable or practical. While it may be difficult to recognize reform when it emerges gradually in a step-by-step fashion, I think that further strengthening of our process of coordination is the best means of achieving further reform of the monetary system.[15]

The deputies decided, for purposes of the study, to divide the issue into three parts: economic policy coordination, exchange rate management, and reserve assets. Each country prepared a position on the issues of greatest interest to it; these individual positions were then synthesized into three informal formulations of issues and options.

Twice during the ensuing months the treasury deputies and their central bank colleagues met to discuss the three issues. Areas of agreement and lack of agreement were identified. These were summarized into an informal report for the ministers and governors, which originally was intended to be written. Extensive revisions submitted by all seven countries to the draft, however, indicated conflicting, irreconcilable views, along the lines outlined above, about the rationale for and conduct of intervention, as well as other aspects of the project. The process was brought to an end rather than a conclusion, with a verbal report to the ministers and governors at the April 1989 ministerial meeting.

Conclusion

The surveillance process developed after the 1986 Tokyo Summit is part of an elaborate institutional framework, but one that has not developed into a real mechanism for economic policy coordination. The analytical framework lends itself best to broad diagnosis of imbalances and exchange rate misalignments and their correction. Without more accurate forecasts and a better understanding of the linkages between goals and instruments, it is question-

---

15. Remarks made at the 1988 International Monetary Conference, Chicago, 6 June 1988.

able whether G-7 surveillance produced any faster or smoother diagnosis or agreement by the participants on, for example, the correct response to a major shock, than less elaborate arrangements would have provided.

Difficulties in establishing policy guidelines and mechanisms for enforcing their use reflected differences about objectives and reticence about using peer pressure. The record of the 1985–89 period suggests a problem of asymmetry in the process: the United States pressed for policy changes by other participants (and used arguments for burden sharing as one rationalization for its own slow progress on fiscal policy change), yet other participants were skeptical of the US administration's ability to deliver on its own promised changes, and therefore they did not always maintain strong counterpressure for remedial US policy action.

Exchange rates attracted more attention than policy changes as a focus for surveillance for several reasons: changes in budget, tax, and structural policies are time consuming to negotiate domestically; when some G-7 participants were slow to deliver, others—especially if they were experiencing similar problems at home—chose not to expose themselves by exerting vigorous peer pressure. These problems meant that exchange market intervention became a relatively attractive instrument, because the participants controlled it directly. Intervention also was perceived to have a signaling impact on exchange rates and conveyed assurances to the markets that something was being done.

Despite the elaborate appearance of the surveillance process, it worked in an informal ad hoc way as time went by, for three reasons:

■ There was no secretariat, no record of decisions, and no institutional memory;
■ The authorities believed they were broadly on the right track to reduce imbalances; although this informal approach seemed to work well with some personalities, the process was vulnerable when they left;
■ Participants differed on the objectives of coordination and the role of the exchange rate as an instrument of adjustment; emphasis on the goal of exchange rate stability and on reference ranges could therefore be used to create the impression of a consensus, which, however, exaggerated the group's ability to deliver.

This informality also allowed other issues—Third World debt strategy, the IMF quota review, and in 1989 the need to respond to developments in

Eastern Europe—to crowd the schedule, leaving insufficient time for surveillance. Although these issues were politically important and the proper domain of treasuries, the large amounts of time spent on them must have reflected the relative political priorities of the participating governments.

What are the prospects for further development of the G-7 process to bring practice more in line with theory? Governments are likely to agree on institutional improvements in the framework for G-7 coordination. They are unlikely to abandon the process, but the level of commitment to ongoing coordination has not been high enough, outside of times of crisis, to invest in a more sophisticated analytical framework. Thus, the level of complexity the process has been able to handle remains far removed from the theoretical approaches of economists.

5 The Impact of Coordination

The business and financial media have paid less attention to the role of macroeconomic policies in G-7 economic policy coordination than to the politics and economics of foreign-exchange market intervention. One reason for this relative neglect is that domestic factors have tended to dominate macroeconomic policy formation, and hence governments are unlikely to acknowledge the role of international peer pressure in this area, even when it helps to convince them to change their ways. Another reason is that the time lag between policy decisions and their impact on the economy tends to be longer than the public's attention span.

Yet both macroeconomic and microeconomic policies have been important objects of the coordination process since 1985. As US Treasury Secretary James A. Baker III pointed out in 1988:

> ... the burden of adjustment is not biased toward or away from domestic policies or exchange rates, as was the case in the par value and early flexible rate regimes, respectively. In 1985 and 1986, coordination stressed the role of exchange rates. In 1987 and so far in 1988, the emphasis has shifted to changes in underlying policies. ...[1]

Hans Tietmeyer, the former German G-7 deputy, has spoken to the same effect:

> ... [G-7 cooperation] is a pragmatic type of cooperation, that attempts to bring economic policies closer into line and, by doing so, contributes toward greater stability in the exchange rate system. It would be wrong—in my view—to focus too much on exchange rates, even if exchange rates can be of high importance in certain situations. The main focus has, of course, to be on underlying policies. ... (Tietmeyer 1988, 140)

This chapter reviews and assesses the impact that G-7 coordination, both of macroeconomic and microeconomic policy changes and of foreign-ex-

---

1. Remarks to the Council on Foreign Relations, Paris, 20 May 1988.

change market intervention, has had on global economic performance since 1985. The first four sections of this chapter assess how national authorities used monetary, fiscal, and structural policies, as well as concerted intervention in foreign-exchange markets, to reduce external imbalances and manage financial crises. Then follows an assessment of the impact of policy coordination: the goals the participants set for the coordination process during the 1985–89 period are revisited and measured against the extent to which they were met. The focus throughout is not only on desirable events that actually occurred but also on undesirable ones that were prevented or averted. The chapter concludes with an attempt to tease apart the separate effects of coordination and other factors on economic performance in the period under study, to determine how much credit coordination can take for the changes that did or did not occur.

Macroeconomic Policy

Fiscal policy adjustment was central to the objective of reducing external imbalances because of its influence both on patterns of growth in domestic demand and output and on saving and investment activity.[2] Fiscal restraint was sought in the United States in particular from mid-decade on, and in other deficit countries such as Canada and Italy as well. Fiscal consolidation in the United States, it was hoped, would slow domestic demand growth, reduce pressures on interest rates, and reduce the attractiveness of the US dollar vis-à-vis the other major currencies and thereby shrink the external deficit. In Canada and Italy, fiscal consolidation was desirable to prevent the emergence of unsustainable external imbalances. Japan and Germany also pursued medium-term fiscal consolidation in the first half of the 1980s, but tackling their large current account surpluses required faster growth of domestic demand than of output, and therefore fiscal stimulus in these countries became a contentious issue in the coordination process later in the decade.

Monetary policy, the chief instrument for achieving and maintaining price stability, is not very useful in reducing current account imbalances because

---

2. Marris's (1987) is the classic analysis of the divergence of national fiscal policies from one another in the first half of the 1980s.

its effects tend to be offsetting. For example, tight US monetary policy could reduce domestic absorption and thus help to reduce the trade deficit, but to the extent interest rates rise and the dollar appreciates as a result, the effect is to hinder the reduction of the trade deficit.

The issues that are central to this analysis are, first, the extent to which the G-7 process increased policymakers' awareness of international spillovers from their domestic policies, and second, the extent to which macroeconomic and microeconomic policy commitments led the G-7 countries to follow different policies, particularly fiscal policies, than they would have followed for good domestic policy reasons alone or because of such macroeconomic concerns as inflation or capacity pressures.

Table 5.1 summarizes the official commitments of individual countries to policy changes in the 1985–89 period. These commitments were made public in official communiqués on three distinct occasions: at the September 1985 Plaza meeting, at the February 1987 Louvre meeting, and following the December 1987 G-7 "telephone accord." Other communiqués from summits and G-7 meetings are not summarized here; they contained more general commitments and views on exchange rates.

MONETARY POLICY

The monetary policy commitments made public in the G-7 process have been relatively few and not very specific, but those that were made have been carried out. In the Plaza Agreement, such commitments related in all cases to the attainment or maintenance of price stability, with the exception of Japan's commitment to pursue a more flexible policy "with due attention to the yen rate." In the Louvre Accord, commitments departed somewhat from domestic preoccupations with price stability: Germany was willing to use monetary policy to improve growth conditions; Japan announced a discount rate reduction. In the December 1987 communiqué, commitments were again very general.

The stance of a country's monetary policy is difficult to quantify. Extensive financial market liberalization during the 1970s and 1980s has made monetary aggregates unstable and hard to interpret. Interest rates, although influenced at the short end of the yield curve by factors such as inflation and output levels, and at the long end by expectations of future inflation, are also directly and profoundly influenced by monetary policy. They are the indica-

T A B L E   5.1   Official policy commitments included in the G-5 and G-7 communiqués, 1985–89

	Fiscal policy	Monetary policy	Structural policy	Trade policy
Plaza Agreement				
France	Curb public expenditure; reduce tax burden; reduce borrowing.	Attain monetary growth targets consistent with decelerating inflation.	Liberalize and modernize financial markets.	Resist protectionist measures.
Germany	Reduce share of public sector in the economy through firm control of public spending.	Ensure stable environment conducive to expansion of domestic demand on a durable basis.	Review labor market policies and practices.	Resist protectionist measures.
Japan	Within the framework for deficit reduction and growth, encourage local governments to invest.	*Exercise flexible management with due attention to the yen exchange rate.*	Apply vigorous deregulation measures; intensify financial market liberalization; open domestic markets.	Resist protectionism. Implement 30 July Action Plan to open markets.
United Kingdom	Reduce public expenditure as a share of GDP; reduce the burden of taxation.	Achieve further progress toward price stability and provide a financial environment conducive to growth.	Privatize public corporations; improve functioning of labor market.	Resist protectionist measures.
United States	Continue efforts to reduce government spending as a share of GNP in order to reduce the fiscal deficit; implement fully the FY1986 deficit reduction package (reduce deficit by over 1 percent of GNP).	Provide a financial environment conducive to sustainable growth and continued progress toward price stability.	Implement tax reform to encourage savings, create work incentives, increase efficiency.	Resist protectionist measures.

FTA = free trade area; FY = fiscal year; italicized items represent policy changes that can be attributed to the coordination process.

TABLE 5.1 Official policy commitments (continued)

	Fiscal policy	Monetary policy	Structural policy	Trade policy
Louvre Accord				
Canada	Progressively reduce fiscal deficit; implement tax reform.	Aim to reduce inflation.	Implement tax reform and regulatory reform; liberalize domestic markets.	Pursue trade liberalization with United States and in Uruguay Round.
France	Reduce central-government deficit by 1 percent of GNP between 1986 and 1988; cut taxes by 1 percent of GNP.		Privatize $6 to $7 billion in government assets; liberalize labor and financial markets.	
Germany	Cut public spending as share of output; reduce tax burden for individuals and corporations; increase tax cuts planned for 1988.	Reduce short-term interest rates; aim at improving conditions for sustained growth while maintaining price stability.	Enhance market forces to foster structural adjustment and innovation.	
Japan	Implement comprehensive tax reform, currently before the Diet, to stimulate economic activity. *Comprehensive program to stimulate demand is under consideration.*	Bank of Japan will reduce discount rate by 0.5 percent.		
United States	Reduce fiscal deficit to 2.3 percent of GNP in FY1988 from 3.9 percent in FY1987; hold growth of government spending below 1 percent in FY1988.	Exercise in a manner consistent with economic expansion at a sustainable, noninflationary pace.	Introduce wide range of policies to improve competitiveness.	

Table continues next page

T A B L E   5.1   Official policy commitments (continued)

	Fiscal policy	Monetary policy	Structural policy	Trade policy
G-7 communiqué, December 1987				
Canada	Continue to reduce fiscal deficit and slow the growth of public debt.	Conduct policy geared to non-inflationary growth.	Implement measures aimed at enhancing competitiveness through tax reform and FTA with the United States.	Intention to implement Canada–US FTA.
France	Reduce fiscal deficit by 0.8 percent of GNP between FY1986 and FY1988; cut taxes by 1.3 percent of GNP. Further tax cuts of 45 billion francs are scheduled for 1989–91.		Continue to carry out 1987 privatization program.	
Germany	Increase tax reductions for 1988 and beyond to DM14 billion; undertake structural tax reform with a further net reduction of DM20 billion from 1990 onward.	Short-term interest rates have been reduced	*Special loans of DM21 billion to be provided for the next 3 years to strengthen private and public investment; accelerate investment in telecommunications infrastructure; deregulate markets further.*	
Italy	Continue progress to correct public-sector imbalances; stabilize debt-GDP ratio.		Devote more resources to financing productive as well as infrastructural investments.	
Japan	¥6 trillion fiscal package is being implemented.	Conduct appropriate and flexible policy supportive of noninflationary growth and exchange rat stability.	Commitments to public works budget in FY1988 to be no less than budget for FY1987.	

T A B L E 5.1 Official policy commitments (continued)

	Fiscal policy	Monetary policy	Structural policy	Trade policy
United Kingdom	Public expenditure growth to increase less rapidly than growth of economy.	Pursue prudent monetary policy.	Take further measures to liberalize markets and promote efficiency.	Continue to work to dismantle trade barriers both in EC and in GATT.
United States	*Bipartisan agreement secured on two-year deficit reduction package. Budget savings to total $76 billion in FY1988 and FY1989.*			Oppose protectionist trade measures.

Sources: Official texts of the communiqués of the meetings.

tor we use here. Interest rate and inflation developments in the G-7 countries between 1984 and 1989 are summarized in tables 5.2 and 5.3, respectively; figure 5.1 presents short-term nominal interest rates in the G-3 countries for the entire decade of the 1980s.

In 1985, the conduct of monetary policy in all of the G-7 countries was consistent with the recovery strategy adopted throughout the OECD after the recession of the early 1980s. US short-term interest rates fell by 2 percentage points between 1984 and the end of 1985; German and Japanese nominal rates, already well below US rates, changed little during this period. In October 1985, however, the Japanese discount rate was raised as part of Japan's Plaza commitment; this move ran counter to domestic preferences but was acknowledged as necessary to head off protectionist sentiment abroad and to put upward pressure on the yen.

March 1986 saw a round of concerted interest rate cuts by central banks in Germany, Japan, and the United States, in the context of lower oil prices and lower inflation. The US Federal Reserve was concerned that these developments not unduly accelerate the dollar's decline. Yet by the summer of 1986, US monetary policy had eased further, because of perceptions of the need for aggregate demand stimulus and the continued absence of inflationary pressures, while the dollar continued its gradual downward trend. Japan, concerned with domestic weakness in response to the strengthening yen, cut its discount rate in October. Highly sensitive to inflationary pressures, Germany resisted further easing of monetary policy after the spring.

In January 1987, continued weakness of the US dollar and upward pressure on the mark and the yen led Germany and Japan to cut their discount rates further. In the months following the February Louvre Accord, monetary policy in Germany and Japan continued to ease. It was now moving in a direction opposite that in the United States, which was tightening in response to interrelated concerns about the continued decline of the dollar, inflationary pressures, and the need to ensure continued inflows of capital from abroad. The German money stock overshot the Bundesbank's target range, while US money supply growth (as measured by M2) was below its target. Inflation fears over the summer led to a rise in the US discount rate in early September, which Japan and Germany later followed, as did a number of other European central banks.

Following the October 1987 stock market collapse, liquidity concerns led to easier monetary policy in the G-7 countries, with cuts in short-term interest rates all around. By spring 1988, however, fears of recession had

TABLE   5.2   Interest rates in the G-7 countries, 1984–89
(percentages per year)

Country	1984	1985	1986	1987	1988	1989
Short-term rates[a]						
Canada	11.2	9.6	9.1	8.4	9.7	12.1
Japan	6.1	6.5	4.9	4.2	4.5	5.3
United States	9.5	7.5	5.9	5.8	6.7	8.1
France	11.7	9.9	7.6	8.3	7.9	9.3
Germany	6.0	5.4	4.6	4.0	4.3	7.1
Italy	17.3	15.3	13.4	11.3	10.8	12.7
United Kingdom	9.3	11.7	10.4	9.7	10.3	13.9
Long-term rates[b]						
Canada	12.7	11.0	9.6	9.9	10.2	9.8
Japan	7.1	6.8	5.8	5.0	4.8	5.2
United States	12.7	11.4	9.0	8.4	8.8	9.2
France	13.4	11.9	8.7	10.2	9.2	9.1
Germany	7.8	7.0	6.0	6.2	6.5	7.0
Italy	15.1	13.1	10.4	10.6	10.5	11.4
United Kingdom	10.7	10.6	9.7	9.6	9.7	10.1

a. Three-month interbank rates except for Canada (90-day finance company paper), the United States (three-month Treasury bills), and Japan (three- to six-month deposit rates).

b. Government, public-sector, and semi-public-sector bonds.

Source: Organization for Economic Cooperation and Development, *OECD Economic Outlook,* various December issues.

TABLE   5.3   Inflation in the G-7 countries, 1984–1989
(percentages per year)[a]

Country	1984	1985	1986	1987	1988	1989
Canada	3.6	3.2	2.9	4.8	4.1	5.3
Japan	1.3	1.5	1.8	−0.3	0.4	1.3
United States	3.9	3.2	2.6	3.0	3.3	4.3
France	7.2	5.7	4.7	2.8	3.2	3.4
Germany	1.9	2.2	3.1	2.5	1.5	2.6
Italy	10.8	8.8	8.0	5.8	6.0	5.7
United Kingdom	4.2	6.0	3.5	4.0	6.6	7.3
Overall	3.7	3.8	3.5	2.6	2.9	3.7

a. Percentage change in the GNP or GDP deflator from the previous year.

Source: Organization for Economic Cooperation and Development, *OECD Economic Outlook,* various December issues.

FIGURE 5.1 Short-term nominal interest rates in the G-3 countries, 1980–90[a]

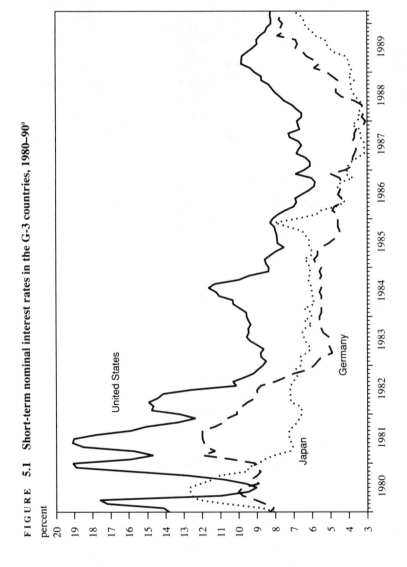

a. Money market rates.

Source: International Monetary Fund, *International Financial Statistics*, various issues.

been replaced by fears of inflation, as stronger-than-expected economic growth occurred in all the OECD countries. Short-term rates now firmed up in the United States, and central banks in several countries were concerned about inflationary pressures and engaged in preemptive tightening. By the summer, having experienced downward pressure on the mark as well as stronger growth in the domestic economy, Germany raised key interest rates. By late 1988 growth of key monetary aggregates had begun to slow in Germany, Japan, and the United States.

In 1989, signs indicated that the previous year's tightening was beginning to slow inflation in the countries at greatest risk, but a firm anti-inflationary stance was maintained in view of still-strong economic activity and rising prices. German interest rates rose significantly, narrowing the interest differential that had favored the US dollar; Japanese rates also rose, but less sharply.

In summary, the 1985–89 period was one of fairly stable inflation in the G-7 countries (as table 5.3 shows), with in fact a slight overall declining trend. The few monetary policy commitments that had been made in the policy coordination process were carried out. Japan, however, may have pursued too much monetary ease after tightening in 1985, as indicated by the gradual rise in the GNP deflator (although still to moderate levels) after 1987. The inflationary consequences for monetary policy of pursuing exchange rate objectives in 1987 also led to increasing wariness, particularly in Germany, of any suggestion that monetary policy might be coordinated in any way, thereby reducing policy independence.

Fiscal Policy

National fiscal stances in the G-7 countries are summarized in table 5.4, which reports fiscal impulse measures for the 1982–90 period, and table 5.5, which compares official national projections of general-government balances (the measure used in G-7 surveillance) with the projections of the international institutions.

Table 5.4 illustrates the wide divergence in fiscal stances in 1985. From 1982 through 1985, the United States and Canada were injecting fiscal stimulus (that is, increasing their deficits), while Italy, Japan, Germany, and the United Kingdom were withdrawing stimulus with the same vigor. (The French fiscal impulse in those years was slightly positive, as was the G-7 average.) These stances were the opposite of what was called for to reduce

T A B L E 5.4 **Fiscal impulse, general government, in the G-7 countries, 1982–89**[a] (percentages of GDP or GNP)

Country	1982	1983	1984	1985	1986	1987	1988	1989	Cumulative 1982–85	Cumulative 1986–89
Canada	1.1	0.9	1.1	1.1	-1.2	-0.8	-0.5	0.5	4.2	-2.0
Japan	-0.5	-0.2	-1.3	-1.0	-0.4	-1.5	-0.9	-0.6	-3.0	-3.4
United States	0.3	0.6	0.7	0.7	0.1	-0.8	0.2	-0.4	2.3	-0.9
France	0.7	0.0	-0.7	0.2	0.0	-0.9	0.4	0.1	0.2	-0.4
Germany	-2.1	-0.4	0.5	-0.1	0.2	-0.5	0.8	-1.7	-2.1	-1.2
Italy	-2.0	-1.4	0.8	0.8	-1.0	-0.6	0.5	-0.6	-1.8	-1.7
United Kingdom	-0.7	0.6	-0.3	-0.5	-0.4	-0.8	-0.9	0.4	-0.9	-1.7
G–7 average	-0.3	0.2	0.2	0.3	-0.1	-0.9	0.0	-0.5	0.4	-1.5

a. A positive (negative) fiscal impulse is defined as an injection (withdrawal) of stimulus. Data are on a national income accounts basis. Composites for the country groups are weighted averages of the individual national ratios for each year, with weights proportionate to the dollar value of the respective GNPs or GDPs in the preceding three years.

Source: International Monetary Fund, World Economic Outlook, December 1990, table A17.

T A B L E   5.5   General-government budget balances in the G-7 countries, projected and actual, 1984–89 (percentages of GDP or GNP)

Country	1984	1985	1986	1987	1988	1989
Canada						
Authorities	−6.9	−7.5	−6.0	−5.4	−4.9	−4.7
IMF	−5.0	−4.6	−4.4	−4.7	−4.1	−3.5
OECD	−5.7	−5.4	−5.5	−4.6	−4.6	−3.4
Actual	−6.5	−6.8	−5.4	−4.0	−2.9	−3.4
Japan						
Authorities	n.a.	n .a.	n.a.	n.a.	n.a.	n.a.
IMF	−3.1	−1.5	−1.6	−2.0	−1.6	−0.1
OECD	−2.5	−0.8	−0.5	−0.4	−0.2	−0.2
Actual	−2.1	−0.8	−0.9	0.7	2.1	2.8
United States[a]						
Authorities	−5.4	−4.6	−4.3	−3.2	−2.3	−2.6
IMF	n.a.	n.a.	−5.0	−3.3	−3.7	−2.6
OECD	n.a.	−4.7	−4.4	−3.8	−3.2	−2.6
Actual	−5.0	−5.4	−5.3	−3.4	−3.2	−3.0
France						
Authorities	−2.9	−3.0	−2.9	−2.5	−2.1	−2.2
IMF	−2.9	−3.3	−3.0	−2.5	−2.1	−2.2
OECD	− 3.1	−0.9	−1.3	−0.4	−2.0	−1.2
Actual	−2.8	−2.9	−2.7	−1.9	−1.8	−1.4
Germany						
Authorities	−1.6	−1.5	−1.0	−1.0	−2.5	−0.5
IMF	−1.9	−1.0	−1.0	−0.8	−2.0	−1.6
OECD	−3.1	−0.9	−1.3	−0.4	−2.0	−1.2
Actual	−1.9	−1.1	−1.3	−1.8	−2.1	0.2
Italy						
Authorities	n.a.	n.a.	n.a.	n.a.	n.a.	n.a.
IMF	−12.5	−12.4	−15.2	−11.1	−9.9	−10.0
OECD	−12.4	−13.1	−13.1	−12.8	−12.2	−9.5
Actual	−11.6	−12.5	−11.7	−11.1	−10.9	−10.2
United Kingdom						
Authorities	−2.3	−2.0	−1.8	−1.0	0.8	2.8
IMF	−2.8	−2.2	−3.1	−2.9	−2.5	0.2
OECD	−2.5	−2.9	−2.9	−3.1	−2.7	0.7
Actual	−3.2	−2.2	−1.3	−0.3	2.2	1.5

n.a. = not available.

a. Actual and authorities' projected data are those for the federal government only and are for fiscal years, whereas OECD and IMF figures are for calendar years.

Sources: See Table 4.3.

the then-existing current account imbalances; thus they indicate the lack of international cooperation in those years.[3]

What connections can be drawn between the coordination process during the 1985–89 period and the changes in fiscal stance that were observed? Initial official commitments to fiscal policy changes were vague, as table 5.1 illustrates. However, by the time of the Louvre meeting in February 1987, some governments were more willing to be specific. The US administration planned to reduce the fiscal deficit to 2.3 percent of GNP by 1988 and to hold the growth of public spending to less than 1 percent of GNP in fiscal year 1988. Germany stated its willingness to increase the tax cuts planned for fiscal 1988; Japan committed itself to consider a comprehensive plan to stimulate domestic demand, which was announced later in the spring and in revised form at the Venice Summit. The French government also made specific commitments, but more as a contribution to the spirit of the process than to its substance; the policy changes themselves were unlikely to influence the central G-7 issue of reducing imbalances.

In December 1987, a number of new commitments were made. The G-7 communiqué issued late that month was triggered by agreement between the US administration and Congress on a budget deficit reduction package intended to ensure that the deficit came in during fiscal 1988 and 1989 at a level $76 billion below what would otherwise have occurred.

United States

In 1985 and 1986, two issues dominated fiscal policy in the United States. One was tax reform: personal and corporate tax bases were widened in 1986 with the adoption of the Tax Reform Act, and rates were lowered. The second was deficit reduction. Although the first Reagan administration in the early 1980s had set a medium-term goal of reducing the size of government, the spending cuts that were achieved were insufficient to offset large cuts in taxes and increases in defense spending.

In December 1985, the Balanced Budget and Emergency Deficit Control Act of 1985, which came to be known as the Gramm-Rudman-Hollings Act

---

3. The OECD has calculated indicators of fiscal stance that, in some cases, differ from these IMF calculations; therefore, caution should be exercised in drawing conclusions from these numbers.

(GRH), was passed and signed into law. This law established steadily declining targets for the deficit after 1986, to culminate in a balanced budget in fiscal 1991. (These targets were revised in the autumn of 1987, to delay the balanced budget until fiscal year 1991, and then abandoned in the autumn of 1990.)

The deficit target for fiscal 1987 was set at $144 billion. Under GRH, unless Congress acted to reduce the projected deficit to this level before the start of the fiscal year in October, any spending beyond the target would be forestalled by sequestering budgetary resources. Except for certain trust and special funds such as Social Security, sequestration was to involve the permanent cancellation of any new budget or other authority to obligate and spend funds.

Passage of GRH was received hopefully, because it seemed to create an impartial mechanism that would force deficit reduction in spite of political pressures to spend or to resist cuts. In reality, however, the law provided a false sense of security. Because the criterion for sequester was a projected rather than an actual deficit figure, no action was necessary even if the actual deficit grossly exceeded the target. This was what happened, leaving an even bigger deficit reduction task for subsequent fiscal years.

For example, whereas the GRH target for 1987 was set at $144 billion, the deficit in fiscal 1986 came in at $220.7 billion, implying the need for $80 billion in deficit reduction in fiscal 1987. The actual 1987 deficit came in at $148 billion, $76 billion below the 1986 peak, because of higher-than-expected revenues related to the introduction of the Tax Reform Act. But the pressures for further policy change after the October stock market collapse led to negotiations between the administration and Congress, which reached agreement on a package of cuts amounting to another $76 billion—that needed to meet the GRH targets in fiscal 1988 and fiscal 1989.

In 1988, the presidential election dominated the policy agenda. The deficit, at $155 billion, was higher than the targeted $144 billion and contributed to growing skepticism that the deficit in future years could be tackled adequately without tax increases.

In November 1989, Congress legislated a $12 billion cut in fiscal 1990 outlays, to meet that year's GRH target of $100 billion, but these cuts were offset by technical revisions, despite the fact that the fiscal 1991 target was $64 billion and would require even larger cuts.

Japan

In Japan, domestic fiscal concerns focused on tax reform and the elimination of bond financing of the deficit. External pressure was building, however, to stimulate growth of domestic demand. This pressure dated back to bilateral discussions in 1986 and early 1987 between Finance Minister Kiichi Miyazawa and US Treasury Secretary James Baker in which Japan sought currency stabilization while the United States sought stimulative fiscal policy in Japan. In early 1987, a special fiscal stimulus package worth ¥5 trillion was introduced, aimed at boosting public works expenditures and lowering income taxes. Shortly before the Venice Summit in June 1987, Prime Minister Yasuhiro Nakasone increased the package to ¥6 trillion.

Analysis of the fiscal record, however, shows that conflicting forces were at work in the conduct of fiscal policy following this commitment. Although public works spending grew rapidly in 1987 and 1988, the general-government deficit was not affected because of higher-than-expected revenues and restrained spending for other current items. The tax reform bill introduced in September 1987, designed to be revenue-neutral when fully implemented in 1989, was actually slightly stimulative because the tax cuts it contained went into effect before the popular tax preferences for interest income from small savings were eliminated.

The fiscal impulse data in table 5.4 must be interpreted with caution because of the sensitivity of the measure to underlying assumptions about potential (which was increasing at the end of the decade); a cautious interpretation would imply neutrality in the 1988–89 period. The general-government budget in table 5.5 was projected to reach near balance by the end of the decade.

Germany

For most of the 1980s, the German authorities also pursued fiscal consolidation. Concerns about structural rigidities in the German economy have contributed to a preoccupation with supply-side measures to stimulate growth. One of these measures was a phased tax reform, which dominated German fiscal policy from its inception in 1986 until it was completed in 1990.

Germany carried out its Louvre Accord commitments to accelerate planned tax cuts, and it introduced an interest subsidy program pledged in December 1987. Because of the nature of federal arrangements in Germany, under which the individual states (Länder) receive a portion of both direct and indirect taxes, carrying out these commitments required a special effort by the federal government to persuade the Länder to agree, in effect, to accelerate the rate at which they were to forgo additional revenue.

The fiscal impulse indicator in table 5.4 shows injection of stimulus occurring in alternate years. The stance of fiscal policy turned restrictive in 1989, with a rise in indirect taxes. Completion of the 1986–90 tax reform and the introduction of a number of other structural reforms were expected to remove economic distortions and contribute to growth and investment in subsequent years.

Other Countries

Canada, France, and Italy all claimed to be pursuing fiscal consolidation during the period under study; table 5.5 shows progress in France and Italy, but ambiguous results for Canada. By 1988, the United Kingdom had moved to a surplus position.

Within the OECD as a whole, growth in 1988 and 1989 was stronger than expected, producing a surge of tax receipts and cyclical improvements through the effect of automatic stabilizers. The OECD countries reported an improved overall budgetary position between 1986 and 1989 of 2 percent of GNP.

Evaluation of Fiscal Policy

The impact of the fiscal policy changes that occurred during the 1985–89 period is summarized in the last two columns of table 5.4, which cumulate the fiscal impulses of those years into two periods. The United States withdrew stimulus marginally in the second period; Germany's stance became less restrictive. Japan's stance in the second period is more difficult to interpret because of the importance of assumptions underlying the fiscal impulse analysis (which may have underestimated economic potential). In light of these uncertainties, it is assumed that there was little change in Japan's stance.

Canada's policy stance showed the largest shift in the correct direction, but the others also moved toward a more prudent stance. Overall, the stance shifted from a slightly stimulative one to a restrictive one.

Comparison of this actual performance with the public commitments made by governments (table 5.1) shows ambiguous results: Japan carried out its

1987 commitments to expand public works spending. Technical analysis, however, suggests that the overall fiscal impact was nearly neutral. This result is surprising in view of the strong growth in domestic demand in 1988 and 1989. Strong private-sector investment was occurring as part of an extensive modernization of plant and equipment, which may have offset continued public-sector saving.

Although the German government resisted committing itself to fiscal stimulus, changes were made that moved Germany in that direction. Tax cuts reflected changes that were already planned for the purpose of simplifying the tax system and increasing its transparency. Tax cuts planned for 1988 were increased in late 1987 as part of the package of policy changes negotiated for the December 1987 policy package. The fiscal impulse indicator for 1988 shows an injection of stimulus.

The pro-growth policies urged on both Japan and Germany were intended to stimulate domestic demand in order to make growth patterns among the three large countries consistent with the reduction of external imbalances. Japan succeeded on this score during the 1985–89 period, whereas Germany did not until early in the 1990s.

The United States did not meet its commitments, but it did withdraw stimulus over the period. The United States committed itself in 1985 to cut the fiscal deficit by 1 percent of GNP; IMF estimates indicate that the central-government deficit–GNP ratio dropped to 4.8 percent in 1986 from 5.3 percent in 1985. The Louvre Accord committed the United States to cut the deficit to 2.3 percent of GNP in fiscal year 1988 from 3.9 percent in fiscal year 1987. The IMF reports that by 1988 the deficit was 3.3 percent of GNP—down from 3.4 percent the previous year, but a full percentage point above the commitment.

The net impact of the 1987 budget summit agreement in the United States has been estimated by the Congressional Budget Office, using its own figures, as follows:

> The total deficit for those two fiscal years [1988 and 1989] turned out to be a total of $59 billion less than the baseline projections that were made immediately after the crash in the stock market in October, 1987. Of this $59 billion difference between forecasts and outcomes, $49 billion was due to policy measures to reduce the deficit. The remainder was due to technical and economic revisions to the original estimates, which turned out to be too pessimistic on balance. (Congressional Budget Office, personal communication)

The failure to fulfill the $76 billion commitment made at the 1987 budget summit can be attributed to two factors: incomplete implementation of the summit agreement, and offsetting increases in the deficit that were enacted in later months in response to new developments. The CBO points out that legislation actually enacted after the budget summit accomplished only $70 billion in cuts[4]; offsetting increases included aid to drought-stricken farmers and spending to deal with thrift insolvencies.

Most of the other countries made general fiscal commitments that reflected ongoing policy thrusts; however, France made a more specific commitment and did reduce its central-government deficit by 1 percent of GNP between 1986 and 1988 as intended. IMF estimates show that the deficit dropped to 1.8 percent in 1988 from 2.8 percent in 1986. These results show what a government can accomplish in the area of fiscal policy when there is a strong political commitment.

Microeconomic Policies

Commitments among the G-7 to change structural policies date back to the Plaza Agreement, where governments agreed to free up market forces through deregulation, privatization, and labor market reform. Explicit trade policy commitments reflected the dominant policy concern with protectionist forces in the US Congress at that time.

In the Louvre Accord, structural policy commitments were less universal, although France put forward a specific commitment, and Canada emphasized the importance it attached to trade liberalization. Japan pledged to ensure that its public works budget in 1988 would be no less than that in 1987. Germany increased its planned tax cuts and stated its intention to stimulate business investment and accelerate infrastructure investment.

Although domestic action to implement these commitments proceeded apace, it was not until 1988 that initiatives were taken in the coordination

---

4. The $6 billion shortfall is accounted for by three factors (reported in Congressional Budget Office 1988, 58–59): a provision in the summit agreement to limit the increase in 1989 appropriations over their 1988 level to less than the rate of inflation was not enacted; asset sales projected in the summit agreement for 1989 were not carried out; and an increase in the tax enforcement effort projected by the summit was not funded.

process to incorporate structural policy more formally into the policy tool kit. The communiqué from the April 1988 ministerial meeting identified the need to give greater attention to structural reform to increase the flexibility of economies and to improve growth and adjustment.

Indeed, the economic rationale for including structural reform in the coordination exercise relates only indirectly to the problem of spillovers. By the mid-1980s it was apparent that greater flexibility in labor and goods markets was a major reason for better economic performance in Japan and the United States than in Europe during the 1983–85 upswing. The greater the contribution of microeconomic policy changes to efficiency and flexibility, the better the allocation of resources and the less need for exchange rate changes to generate a given amount of adjustment.

Another reason for the increased attention to structural reform was that the political climate was favorable to it. Ministerial meetings in 1988 were rather low-key affairs compared to those of the previous year. Growth was stronger than expected. The United States was gearing up for a presidential election. US representatives to the G-7 noted that structural reform had received little systematic attention in the process and suggested taking advantage of this breathing space to remedy that shortcoming.

The issue became a focus for ministers and leaders at the Toronto Summit; there an annex was attached to the communiqué detailing respective national commitments in the area of structural reform (table 5.6). Governments implemented reforms in four areas:

- Improved incentives to work, save, and invest;
- Removal of barriers, controls, and regulations;
- Increased exposure to market competition;
- Enhanced human resource development.

During the 1980s, most of the G-7 countries have implemented tax reforms with the goal of increasing private-sector incentives, broadening tax bases, and lowering tax rates. Deregulation and elimination of controls have also been widespread, especially in financial markets, where technological change and globalization have made the costs of regulation more apparent. Most of the seven have privatized some state-owned industries to increase exposure to market competition. With the notable exception of agriculture, each of the three largest countries has undertaken measures to reduce support payments and direct subsidies.

Measures to enhance human resource development have varied widely, reflecting differences in the structure of labor markets. There have been, however, two common strands to policy: first, government programs have emphasized training to increase mobility and wage flexibility, and, second, pension and social security reforms have been emphasized in light of anticipated demographic developments.

Structural reform did not become a full-fledged part of the coordination exercise for several reasons. First, policy commitments take time to implement and are difficult to track and evaluate. Second, there has been considerable skepticism about the impact of reforms in this area on current account adjustment, particularly in Germany. In theory, such changes should raise German incomes and employment. But while a wealthier Germany might buy more from the rest of the world, a more efficient Germany could also be expected to export more.

Attempts were made at three G-7 deputies' meetings in the summer and autumn of 1988 to extend the surveillance process to structural reforms. On the principle that peer review can assist countries in undertaking policy reforms that might be unpopular in an exclusively domestic perspective, it might have been expected that participants would agree to periodic scrutiny of commitments and of progress in their implementation.

After these discussions, however, it became apparent that jurisdictional issues hampered ministers in Germany and Japan—in the latter case, according to one Ministry of Finance official, the Finance Minister encountered public criticism for exceeding his mandate in discussing structural issues at the spring ministerial meeting (personal communication). The argument was made that ministers can only make commitments in the coordination process that they have direct responsibility to implement.

Because of these constraints, consideration of structural reform was confined to areas such as the financial sector, where all the ministers involved in the G-7 have direct responsibility. The issues in bilateral Japan–US relations were subsequently addressed in the bilateral Structural Impediments Initiative, which was closely directed in its later stages by both President George Bush and Prime Minister Toshiki Kaifu. The broader analytical and political focus was sought at the OECD, where a larger number of ministerial jurisdictions could be represented to address these issues.

TABLE 5.6 Official commitments by the G-7 countries to structural reforms, 1985–89

Country	Plaza Agreement, September 1985	Louvre Accord, February 1987	G-7 communiqué, December 1987	Toronto Summit, June 1988	OECD Ministerial, May–June 1989
Canada		Implement tax reform and regulatory reform; liberalize domestic markets.	Implement tax reform and Canada–US FTA to enhance competitiveness.	Tax reform stage 2; implement financial services reform; implement Canada–US FTA.	Control public debt; introduce GST, UI reform; reduce barriers to interprovincial trade.
France	Liberalize and modernize financial markets.	Liberalize labor and financial markets; privatize $6 to $7 billion in government assets.	Privatization being carried out; sustain household savings; develop competitive financial markets; improve competitiveness of firms.	Improve education and professional training of workers; improve financial market functioning to raise savings and lower costs.	Increase competition; reduce budget deficit; remove exchange controls.
Germany	Review labor market policies and practices.	Enhance market forces to foster structural adjustment and innovation.	Strengthen business investment with special loan program; accelerate investment in telecommunications infrastructure; deregulate markets further.	Implement tax reform; deregulate; privatize; reform telecommunications system; increase labor market flexibility; reform social security system.	Reform social security; continue tax reform; reform telecommunications; increase flexibility of work time; reemploy jobless; change transportation regulations; change store closing hours.
Italy			Devote more resources to financing productive as well as infrastructural investments.	Promote training and education; increase labor market flexibility and functioning of financial markets.	Reduce fiscal deficit by 50 percent; implement tax reform; increase labor market mobility; increase public-private sector coordination.

TABLE 5.6 **Official commitments by the G-7 countries to structural reforms, 1985–89** (continued)

Country	Plaza Agreement, September 1985	Louvre Accord, February 1987	G-7 communiqué, December 1987	Toronto Summit, June 1988	OECD Ministerial, May-June 1989
Japan	Apply vigorous deregulation measures; intensify financial market liberalization; open domestic markets.		Commitments to public works budget in FY1988 to be no less than budget for FY1987.	Increase domestic demand; reform land use; change distribution system; continue tax reform.	Change tax system to anticipate demographic changes; reform land use; take measures in construction, transport, and financial sectors to increase market access.
United Kingdom	Privatize public corporations; improve functioning of labor market.	Cut tax burden and public spending as share of GDP; privatize.	Take further measures to liberalize markets and promote efficiency.	Continue tax reform; reform trade unions; deregulate; privatize; improve quality of education and flexibility of labor markets.	Balance budget in medium term; increase competition; reform restrictive trade practices; continue tax reform; provide employment training; improve education standards; reduce regulatory burden on business.
United States	Implement tax reform to encourage savings, create work incentives, increase efficiency.	Intends to introduce wide range of policies to improve competitiveness and enhance strength and flexibility of economy.		Increase incentives to save; strengthen international competitiveness.	Contain inflation; reduce budget deficit (eliminate by 1993); deal with problems of financial institutions.

FTA = free trade area; GST = goods and services tax; UI = unemployment insurance.

Sources: Official texts of the communiqués of the meetings.

Foreign-Exchange Market Intervention

The views and commitments of the G-7 countries in the area of foreign-exchange market intervention (table 4.8) have been much more specific than their commitments involving either macroeconomic or microeconomic policy (table 5.1). This difference reflects the treasuries' perception of their greater control over this policy instrument. The focus of this concern, the trends in yen-dollar and mark-dollar exchange rates, is summarized for the 1985–90 period in figure 5.2.

TYPES OF INTERVENTION AND THEIR EFFECTS

Intervention by national authorities in the foreign-exchange markets affects exchange rates in two ways: through a portfolio balance effect and through a signaling effect. In the latter, intervention affects exchange rate expectations by indicating (signaling) to the markets the authorities' future policy intentions. The portfolio balance effect, on the other hand, works by affecting the relative supply of bonds denominated in different currencies. Economists have sought to measure both effects on foreign-exchange market behavior to determine whether, to what extent, and under what circumstances they actually occur.

Intervention can be sterilized or unsterilized. In sterilized intervention, official purchases or sales of foreign currencies are offset by domestic transactions, so as to leave the monetary liabilities of both home and foreign authorities unchanged.[5] The virtue of sterilized intervention as an instrument derives from the fact that it does not conflict with other policy objectives, although it can affect the stock of foreign-exchange reserves. It also has the advantage of being a fast and easy way to convey signals about future policy intentions to financial markets. Information that the authorities are intervening, or planning to intervene, in support of a currency, for example, can

---

5. Sterilization in this example works by changing the currency denomination of bonds held by the public. If a central bank buys foreign currency, it thereby increases its holdings of foreign assets. Such a purchase would reduce private-sector holdings of foreign assets and increase private-sector holdings of the home currency. This increase has the effect of expanding the monetary base unless the central bank removes an equivalent amount from the market by, for example, selling an equivalent amount of own-currency-denominated bonds to the public.

FIGURE 5.2 Nominal yen-dollar and mark-dollar exchange rates, 1985–90[a]

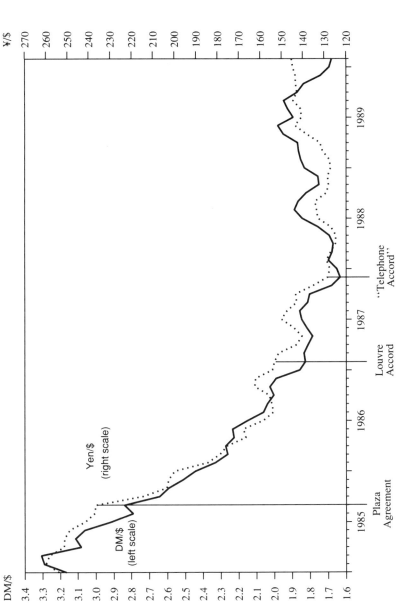

a. Monthly averages.

Source: Wharton Econometrics Forecasting Associates data base.

cause speculators to expect an increase in the future price of that currency. Unsterilized intervention, on the other hand, achieves more than a signaling effect because it affects the size of the money supply; this implies that unsterilized intervention is more likely to conflict with other policy objectives, particularly that of controlling inflation.

Most of the available evidence has tended to support the conclusion that sterilized intervention may have a temporary signaling effect, but by itself has no lasting effect on exchange rates. Two official reports in the early 1980s came to this conclusion. In 1983, the Working Group on Exchange Market Intervention concluded (in its Jurgensen Report) that sterilized intervention has a much smaller exchange rate impact than unsterilized intervention, and that sterilized intervention can have some short-run impact and may therefore be effective in achieving some short-run objectives, but that it does not appear to have any long-run impact on exchange rates unless it complements and supports other policies (Working Group on Exchange Market Intervention 1983). In 1985, deputies of the Group of Ten looking at the performance of floating exchange rates endorsed the 1983 conclusions in their final report, and observed that official intervention can play a role in reducing exchange rate volatility (Group of Ten 1985).

Feldstein (1986) and Obstfeld (1990) have assessed G-5 and G-7 intervention at different times during the 1985–88 period. Feldstein claimed that the G-5's intervention in the currency markets after the Plaza meeting in 1985 had no impact on the dollar's decline; Obstfeld concluded that monetary and fiscal policy played a more important role in determining currency relationships than did intervention.

The literature thus makes an important distinction between the long-term and the short-term (signaling) impact of intervention. Bergsten (1986) pointed out that the short-term effects can be significant; he argued that price setting in exchange markets is dominated by changes in expectations and risk premia rather than by demand for and supply of financial assets. The prospect of coordinated intervention by central banks in the large countries can change these expectations or at least the perceived risks of holding individual currencies. This impact seems particularly likely when a government is thought to be committed to reducing rather than defending the value of its own currency. Bergsten has pointed out that when markets are already pushing currency relationships in the direction of equilibrium, joint intervention by "leaning with the wind" can promote needed adjustment through signaling effects.

Edison (1990), in a survey of the literature, reports that most researchers have found neither a quantitatively nor a statistically significant effect of sterilized intervention on the exchange rate. Descriptive studies (Edison 1990) have concluded that sterilized intervention has had a temporary impact and has been a useful short-run tool to stabilize trading conditions and to provide time for policy adjustments to occur.

Dominguez and Frankel (1990) have carried out a sophisticated analysis of the effect of intervention on the exchange rate. Using daily dollar-mark intervention data from the Bundesbank during the mid-1980s and newspaper reports of actual intervention and of relevant statements by officials, as well as data on investors' expectations, they found statistically (but not quantitatively) significant effects through both the signaling and the portfolio channels. They also paid particular attention to distinguishing between public and secret intervention and found that, during the sample period, intervention had to be publicly known for the magnitude of the effects to be large.

FIVE EPISODES OF INTERVENTION

Since the nominal value of the US dollar reached its 1980s peak in 1985 (figure 5.2), there have been five episodes during which intervention by national authorities has been heavy and concerted. These episodes are clearly seen in table 5.7, which reports net intervention purchases by the US authorities (comparable data for intervention operations by the monetary authorities in the other major countries are not available). This concerted intervention is distinct from actions taken to smooth out market fluctuations. Each of the five episodes is examined below in terms of the behavior of nominal exchange rates during the episode, the goals and use of intervention, and the conduct of monetary policy. This analysis illustrates some of the difficulties of arriving at a definitive conclusion without more rigorous analytical techniques such as those employed by Dominguez and Frankel. In most episodes, the impact of intervention cannot be disentangled from other changes, including monetary and fiscal policy changes and improvements in the US external balance.

Episode 1: September 1985–February 1987

The key time period in this episode was the last quarter of 1985, when

FIGURE 5.3 Episode 1: G-3 nominal exchange rates and interest rate differentials,[a] September 1985–February 1987

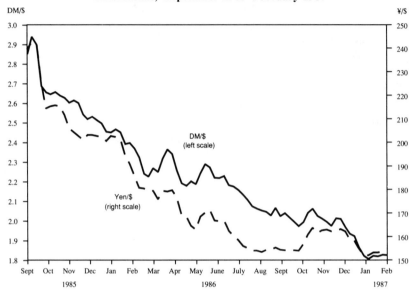

Exchange rates

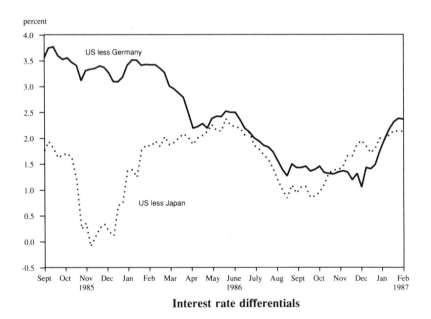

Interest rate differentials

a. Weekly averages. Interest rate differentials are based on Eurocurrency rates.

Source: Wharton Econometrics Forecasting Associates data base.

intervention was heavy (figure 5.3). The goal of intervention had been set at the September Plaza meeting: to lean with the wind, accelerating the downward pace of the already-declining US dollar. Large-scale intervention occurred in the month after the meeting. The nominal value of the dollar dropped sharply just after the meeting and continued to fall through the spring of 1986. At that time, officials began to express reservations about the dollar's continued decline, and authorities in the non–US industrial countries intervened heavily to support it. The US authorities were not involved at this juncture (table 5.7), which suggests that the other countries were trying to prevent the appreciation of their own currencies.

Nominal short-term US interest rates were much higher than those in Germany in late 1985, but this differential narrowed sharply in 1986 (reducing the relative attractivness of dollar-denominated financial assets). At that time a coordinated round of discount rate cuts occurred, designed to slow upward pressure on the mark and the yen. In a retrospective analysis of the May 1986–February 1987 period, the IMF reported that one of the main

T A B L E   5.7   **Net foreign-exchange intervention by US authorities, by month, 1985–89** (millions of US dollars)[a]

Month	1985	1986	1987	1988	1989
January	−94.0	0.0	50.0	715.0	−1,880.0
February	−479.4	0.0	0.0	0.0	−350.0
March	−85.6	0.0	1,884.0	0.0	−1,519.0
April	0.0	0.0	2,150.0	0.0	−270.0
May	0.0	0.0	293.0	0.0	−6,735.0
June	0.0	0.0	513.0	−480.0	−4,952.0
July	0.0	0.0	0.0	−2,420.0	−230.0
August	0.0	0.0	−367.0	−1,806.0	−1,020.0
September	−230.5	0.0	119.0	−330.0	−3,102.4
October	−2,968.2	0.0	432.0	200.0	−1,748.6
November	−102.2	0.0	1,149.0	2,141.0	−75.0
December	0.0	0.0	2,276.0	259.0	−75.0

a. Purchases (sales) of dollars are represented by positive (negative) numbers. ·

Source: Federal Reserve Bulletin (FRB), various issues; and IMF staff estimates (in allocating data between calendar months when FRB does not do so).

factors slowing the decline of the dollar in this period was the perception that US monetary policy might have become more restrictive in response to increasing inflationary pressures (International Monetary Fund 1988). Yet interest differentials continued to move against the dollar until the autumn of 1986, when Japanese and German discount rates were lowered. Except for a brief rise against the yen, the dollar continued its downward trend.

Episode 2: February–September 1987

Japanese and German concerns about the domestic impact of their strong currencies, together with US concerns about the need to continue to attract capital flows from abroad at reasonable interest and exchange rates, figured strongly in the Louvre meeting on 22 February 1987. At that meeting a common commitment to seek greater exchange rate stability was concluded. In the ensuing months, authorities of several G-7 countries, including the United States, engaged in large-scale intervention, the need for which was exacerbated by market uncertainties about US–Japanese trade frictions.

Between mid-March and mid-April, the dollar continued to decline against the yen despite heavy concerted intervention (figure 5.4); this eventually led to the rebasing of the yen-dollar reference range in April. The dollar-mark relationship was relatively stable throughout this period. The dollar strengthened against both currencies in the May–August period.

Monetary policy in Japan and Germany moved in a direction opposite that in the United States, with those two countries easing while the United States tightened. Interest rate differentials moved against the dollar during the summer, but by September interest rates had increased in all three countries in response to domestic inflationary concerns. The US Treasury authorities, concerned that the burden of current account adjustment was not being shared by others, questioned the rationale for the foreign interest rate increases and publicly worried about the breakdown in coordination.

Episode 3: Post–October 1987

Following the stock market crash of mid-October 1987 (the crisis itself is the subject of the next section), exchange rate relationships initially were unaffected. But the dollar soon resumed its decline; from average bilateral values of DM1.80 and ¥143 in September and October, the dollar fell to an average of DM1.68 and ¥135 by November despite substantial intervention (figure

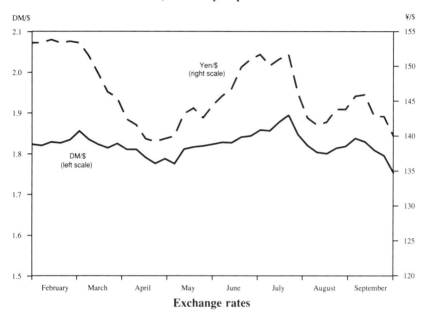

Exchange rates

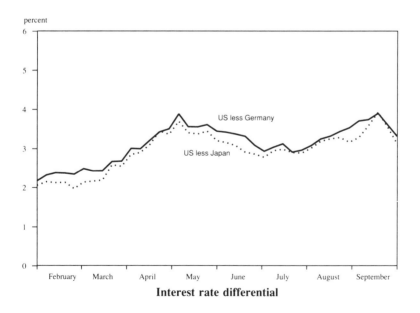

Interest rate differential

a. Weekly averages. Interest rate differentials are based on Eurocurrency rates.

Source: Wharton Econometric Forecasting Associates data base.

5.5). The IMF (1988, 59) chronicled the negative factors seen to be influencing market sentiment at that time: negative interpretations of the 20 November congressional agreement on US budget deficit reduction; declining oil prices; worsening US trade figures; and uncertainty about the intentions of the G-7.

Heavy intervention occurred in late December and early January 1988 following issuance of the 22–23 December G-7 communiqué; its purpose was to bridge to anticipated improvements in the US trade figures, which indeed began to materialize in February 1988. The sharp response in the foreign-exchange markets, particularly in the yen-dollar relationship, in the first days of 1988 is apparent in figure 5.5.

Monetary policy during this period included interest rate reductions in response to the stock market collapse. Wider interest rate differentials slowly began to favor the US dollar, but it was not until March that the US authorities began to raise interest rates, after the dollar had risen from its low at the end of the year. The major currencies fluctuated in narrow ranges throughout the period between January and June 1988.

Episode 4: June–September 1988

In mid-June a new phase of dollar appreciation began as evidence continued to appear of an improving US trade balance and as dollar interest rates firmed. From average levels of DM1.69 and ¥124 in May, the dollar appreciated to averages of DM1.88 and ¥133 in August (figure 5.6).

Intervention, particularly by the US and German central banks, continued throughout the summer. The dollar failed to stabilize against the mark until the end of August after the Bundesbank raised its discount rate, reducing slightly the interest differential favoring the dollar. Thereafter, with the exception of a period of dollar weakness late in the year, currencies fluctuated little until the spring of 1989.

Episode 5: March–October 1989

In the spring of 1989, the dollar began to strengthen again; this trend persisted until late in the year (figure 5.7). The strong market sentiment favoring the dollar puzzled the authorities, since it was not consistent with medium-term economic fundamentals, at least as measured in nominal terms. Conflicting public statements by the authorities during May and June contrib-

FIGURE 5.5 Episode 3: G-3 nominal exchange rates and interest rate differentials,[a] October 1987–January 1988

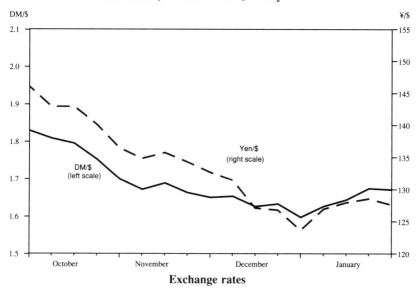

Exchange rates

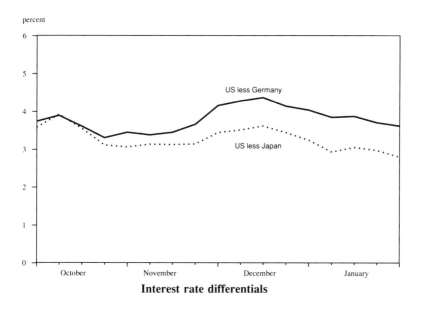

Interest rate differentials

a. Weekly averages. Interest rate differentials are based on Eurocurrency rates.

Source: Wharton Econometrics Forecasting Associates data base.

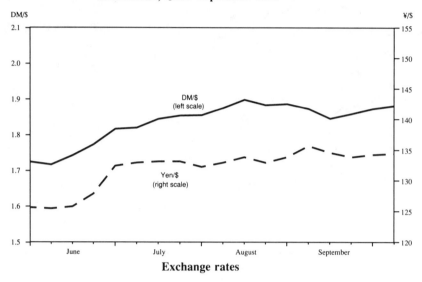

Exchange rates

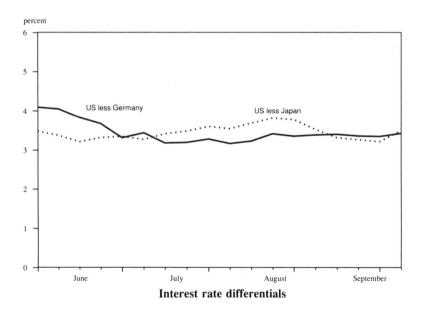

Interest rate differentials

a. Weekly averages. Interest rate differentials are based on Eurocurrency rates.

Source: Wharton Econometric Forecasting Associates data base.

FIGURE 5.7 Episode 5: G-3 nominal exchange rates and interest rate
differentials,[a] March–October 1989

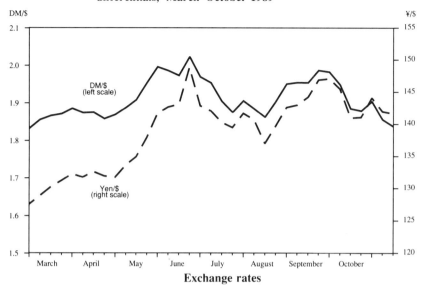

Exchange rates

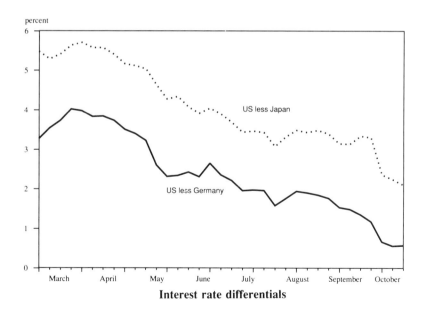

Interest rate differentials

a. Weekly averages. Interest rate differentials are based on Eurocurrency rates.

Source: Wharton Econometric Forecasting Associates data base.

uted to a growing perception that the coordination process had broken down.

Economic fundamentals did not favor the dollar. Nominal interest differentials favoring the dollar were narrowing throughout this period from high levels the year before, and a US economic slowdown was expected as a result of a combination of tighter US monetary and fiscal policy stances. Although the average OECD inflation rate seemed fairly stable at around 4 percent, rising demand pressures in Germany and Japan resulted in discount rate increases in both countries during the spring and summer that narrowed the short-term interest differential. Real interest rate differentials, however, may not have been narrowing by as much as nominal differentials during this period if inflation was expected to accelerate faster abroad than in the United States. In Japan, a marked decline of the current account surplus was seen to contribute to the yen's weakness.

A number of noneconomic factors could be identified as influencing market sentiment: these included greater political uncertainties in both Germany and Japan than in the United States, and negative sentiment generated by the Tiananmen Square massacre in Beijing in early June. Expectational factors played a role as well; optimism grew about the prospect of a soft landing for the US economy and continued progress on reduction of the trade deficit.

Intervention by the authorities was heavy during May and June (table 5.7), but not always concerted among the three major countries. Intervention activity declined during July and August and then intensified again shortly after the September 1989 ministerial meeting in Washington.

The dollar declined slightly against both the mark and the yen in the period immediately following the meeting. Thereafter, however, the yen's weakness continued; the mark meanwhile continued to strengthen throughout the rest of the year as rapid political change in Eastern Europe positively affected European economic prospects, particularly in Germany.

Official views differed about the potential impact of intervention. One argument focused on the need to preserve the alleged reference ranges; this view reflected a strong concern about the need to "follow the rules" in order to preserve the credibility of coordination. The other argument focused on the need to understand the economic (and noneconomic) fundamentals. It was felt that intervention in the face of very strong opposite market sentiment would be costly, in terms of both reserves and credibility.

Actions of the central banks were important in this episode because of the potential conflict between domestic and international objectives. Minutes of the 3 October 1989 meeting of the Federal Open Market Committee report a discussion about easing monetary policy. Concern was expressed " . . . that an easing of policy so soon after the G-7 meeting would be misinterpreted as an attempt to use monetary policy to force the dollar lower."[6]

The Fed was not the only central bank concerned about such a linkage. Although treasury officials were aware of (and some were sympathetic to) the central banks' concerns about linkage, another issue was which country should be responsible for moving interest rates. Europeans were concerned about possible repercussions within the EMS if the Bundesbank (and Japan) raised interest rates, but they also pointed out an asymmetry in financial markets. Raising rates in Germany and Japan, it was argued, would impress the market less than would lowering US rates.

Another factor was skepticism among some participants about the impact of intervention. Those who believed that the impact was mainly on expectations also believed it should reliably indicate future changes in policy.[7] Yet prospects for progress on the US fiscal deficit were deteriorating. This could mean that pressure for change in monetary policies would build. In such a situation, prudence suggested that intervention should not be undertaken until or unless changes in monetary policy were required for domestic reasons. A confluence of such factors seemed to appear in the September-October period, which contributed to a willingness to engage in concerted intervention after the September 1989 ministerial meeting. The purpose of this intervention was to signal the view, expressed in the communiqué, that the dollar's strength was not consistent with medium-term economic fundamentals.

---

6. *Federal Reserve Bulletin*, January 1990, 20.

7. Peter Kenen has pointed out to me a defect in the conventional formulation of this signaling argument: the view that intervention should not be undertaken unless it can be interpreted (correctly) as a signal about future policy makes sense if and only if markets base their own exchange rate expectations on their views about future policy fundamentals. If markets are dominated by "chartists," however, intervention may be deemed to signal official views about the appropriateness of exchange rates without necessarily signaling the manner in which governments intend to influence the situation in the medium term; intervention may be taken to signal more massive intervention, which may be enough to influence expectations—and therefore exchange rates.

Did Concerted Intervention Work?

This survey of five episodes of concerted intervention in the 1985–89 period illustrates the difficulties involved in distinguishing the effects of sterilized intervention from the effects of monetary policy changes that might have occurred anyway. It is also difficult to disentangle other influences affecting both the risk preferences of assetholders and market sentiment, such as perceptions of the intentions of the monetary authorities, and perceptions of progress (or lack thereof) in the adjustment of US current account imbalances.

The effects of intervention in the five episodes can be summarized as follows:

■ The goal of the Plaza Agreement to accelerate the decline of the dollar was met; intervention had an immediate impact on the dollar, which fell 4 percent in the days immediately after the meeting; this intervention was regarded by many to have been a factor in the substantial decline in the dollar through early 1987.

■ One goal of the Louvre Accord was to stabilize the dollar. Intervention was directed to this goal, as to some extent were changes in monetary policy, although inflation concerns in the United States were also very real. Some degree of stability was achieved, but the authorities set the reference range for the dollar at a higher level than would be consistent with slower growth in US domestic demand and declining US fiscal and trade deficits. Instead of rebasing the range as the months went by, the US Treasury attempted to maintain—for too long, as it turned out—existing interest rate differentials in order to maintain the range.

■ In the episode following the collapse in world stock prices in October 1987, the goal of concerted and aggressive intervention, which some have dubbed the "bear trap," was to stabilize the dollar following publication of macroeconomic and structural policy commitments in the 22–23 December G-7 communiqué. This goal was achieved: concerted intervention was successful in restoring the authorities' credibility. This may in turn have been a factor influencing stability in markets in subsequent months. The lowering of German interest rates late in 1987 also contributed to a change in interest differentials that began to favor the dollar.

■ In the summer of 1988, the authorities set out to stabilize the rising dollar. Intervention was undertaken by US and German authorities, and German interest rates rose. The interest differential moved against the dollar. The dollar began to stabilize in August.

The evidence from these episodes adds to the existing anecdotal evidence reported by Edison (1990) that sterilized intervention can have an effect if the authorities' signals of future policy adjustments are perceived to be serious, as was the case in 1985, late 1987, and early 1988. Their failure in 1987 to follow their signal from the Louvre meeting with the required policy adjustments undermined the credibility of this instrument and of the coordination process.

The verdict on the 1989 episode is less supportive of the effectiveness of concerted intervention. Intervention together with changes in interest differentials had some effect in June on the dollar's relationships to the mark and yen, but the effect did not last. Strong market sentiment favoring the dollar persisted. Further concerted intervention following the G-7 ministerial and communiqué in late September 1989 again had a temporary effect: even though changes in interest rates in the three major countries in October moved in directions unfavorable to the dollar, the yen continued to weaken against the dollar.

IMPLICATIONS

Behind these five episodes, the tactics of intervention were evolving in response to the tension between rules and pragmatism described in chapter 4. By 1989, the pragmatic view prevailed that intervention be related to economic fundamentals rather than to mechanistic ranges. The consensus view that these fundamentals implied that the dollar should be lower was signaled with some success in September 1989, by means of an official G-7 statement followed by concerted intervention. Subsequent interest rate changes also supported this view in that differentials narrowed, reducing the relative attractiveness of dollar-denominated assets.

Greater flexibility in the use of the reference range concept emerged over the 1985–89 period, with a widening of the ranges in 1988 and 1989. Some participants argued for such flexibility to take account of market sentiment and to ensure that intervention contained an element of surprise, which was felt to be an important ingredient in successfully reducing destabilizing speculation. This view, however, has its critics, who believe that the effectiveness of intervention would be increased if governments announced their reference ranges in a forthright way. These critics also argue that, by concealing their views, the G-7 governments squandered their credibility, as it became increasingly came to appear that markets, not governments, influenced exchange rates.

Support grew for more regular consultations, which were felt necessary to carry forward the more pragmatic approach to exchange rate management. The need for a better understanding of monetary and interest rate developments, particularly in 1989, indicated the desirability of involving the central bank deputies. Considerable agreement also emerged on the need for "verbal discipline"—that is, less public comment from individual participants and avoidance of conflicting public statements. Nonetheless, differences between treasuries and central banks continued to surface periodically in the United States, and the public airing of differences between the Bank of Japan and the Japanese Ministry of Finance in spring 1990 indicated that this principle was not fully in practice in that country either.

Crisis Management

The October 1987 stock market crash tested the cooperative abilities of the G-7 participants, but also provoked criticism from those who saw coordination as itself a causal factor in the crisis.[8] Although the public airing of policy disagreements between the United States and Germany was indeed the immediate cause of the crisis, the underlying cause was the speculative bubble in stock market prices throughout many of the preceding months in 1987. The crisis was simply waiting for a trigger.

When the crisis came, it provided an opportunity to test the ability of the G-7 to manage such crises successfully. Most of the G-7 central banks responded quickly (the Bundesbank responded with a lag), pumping liquidity into the system to offset the potential deflationary impact of the fall in stock prices. Treasury ministers and deputies were in constant touch with each other, with their central bank colleagues, and with market participants. That these extensive communications were able to take place relatively smoothly

---

8. Events leading up to the 1987 crash have been analyzed elsewhere. An early analysis is that of Morgan Guaranty Trust Company (1987). One that focuses on the international factors is that by Frankel (forthcoming).

was one of the great benefits of regular G-7 meetings in preceding years and other investments in building familiarity among the players. The picture of the crisis that quickly emerged was that damage was extensive but confined to the financial markets. Governments and central banks were able to work on restoring public confidence.

In the background, discussion was intense about what had to be done (including restoring credibility to the coordination process). There was a consensus that until a policy package could be assembled, a ministerial meeting would be counterproductive. Peer pressure was used with some effect on US policymakers, on whom it was impressed that the centerpiece of the package had to be a credible US deficit reduction commitment. Given the constraints imposed by the approaching 1988 presidential campaign, it was realized that implementation of the package would have to be stretched over two years. For its part, the US administration was willing to embark on such a quest with Congress, but it was also determined that the burden of policy adjustment should be shared by all the G-7 participants.

These discussions about substance were accompanied by media-generated speculation about process, such as the prospect of an emergency ministerial meeting. Ignored was the reality that the substance of any ministerial agreement had to be developed first in national capitals, and only then internationally, and finally through an iteration between the two levels.

Senior officials in the Reagan administration became engaged in active negotiations with Congress in November. At that point, the focus of communications among the G-7 shifted to the policy changes other countries would be prepared to make. Major contributions included German commitments to increase domestic investment, and US and Japanese commitments to fiscal policy restraint and stimulus, respectively (see emphasis in table 5.1).

The other subject of intense international discussion at this time was foreign-exchange market intervention. Although central banks engaged in smoothing operations, little was done initially to influence the level of the US dollar. Surprising as this might have seemed to market participants at the time, the rationale was quite consistent with the broader interpretation of the Louvre Accord, namely, to make policy changes that would be consistent with stable currencies. US fiscal policy change consistent with exchange rate stability had been the missing ingredient in the period between February and October. It was felt that both policy changes and exchange rate changes should be used as channels of adjustment, with exchange rates allowed to change at least until the policy package had been assembled and implemented.

This was the strategy that was followed. It took until late December for the US administration to reach an accord with Congress on a two-year deficit reduction package. Late on 22 December (North American time; it was already 23 December in Japan) a G-7 communiqué was released. Following the Louvre framework, it contained policy commitments and a renewed agreement on exchange rates. Like the rebasing agreement with Japan in April 1987, the December agreement was also a rebasing that accepted market-determined exchange rate relationships. This meant that the range for intervention became one that allowed the dollar to rise as long as it did not undermine the adjustment process.

Skeptical comments by some senior US officials in December contributed to continuing financial market uncertainty. Market participants tested the commitment of authorities to the accord by selling the US dollar around the end of the year. Central banks moved aggressively and in concert into the market in late December. Operations occurred around the globe and around the clock. It soon became clear that the central banks had changed their tactics. The dollar reached its low in the first week of January, and heavy intervention to support it continued through mid-January.

The rationale for intervention was to bridge to some better US trade balance reports, which were expected on the basis of longer-term trends under way in the US economy. This rationale proved sound. By February 1988 evidence of adjustment began to appear in the US trade balance, which gained surprisingly strong momentum as the year progressed.

In summary, the authorities passed the test of rapid response to the crisis, even if their accomplishments were modest. Central bankers have insisted since the crisis that their close cooperation with each other would have happened whether or not the G-7 mechanism had existed. Yet the crisis also induced adoption of a package of mutually beneficial policy changes, most of which were implemented. The US budget accord, which prevented the deficit from rising even further, might not have happened in the absence of the G-7 framework. Some stimulative changes were made in German policy as well: the December policy package provided the basis for concerted intervention that accomplished the limited goals set for it.

The Impact of Policy Coordination

This examination of the impact of policy coordination is divided into two parts. The first is an objective assessment of the extent to which the economic goals set in the coordination process were actually achieved. The second attempts to distinguish the role coordination itself played in achieving those goals from the effects of other factors already at work. There we focus on the influences of the policy coordination process on domestic policy formation, and consider what might have happened in its absence.

WERE THE ECONOMIC GOALS MET?

Three main economic goals were identified in the coordination process:

- To reduce current account imbalances to sustainable levels;
- To change the pattern of output and domestic demand growth in the surplus and deficit countries;
- To realign the US dollar against the mark and the yen, and then to stabilize its nominal value within ranges against these currencies.

Another goal, which does not lend itself easily to objective evaluation, was to promote structural reform. Last but not least, an implicit objective was to sustain noninflationary world growth.

The record summarized below is one of partial success in meeting the three main goals. Current account imbalances were reduced in the United States and Japan, but Germany's surplus widened. Economic analysts retained serious doubts at the end of 1989 as to the medium-term sustainability of current account imbalances. Patterns of growth in output and domestic demand were changed in Japan and the United States, but not in Germany. The goal of accelerating the decline of the US dollar was met, and the dollar was subsequently stabilized within a wide range in the 1988–89 period. It dropped further in 1990 in response to changes in the medium-term economic fundamentals.

Reducing Current Account Imbalances

Data on current account and trade balances, compiled by the G-7 countries themselves (which are the data the participants used in monitoring), were presented in tables 4.5 and 4.6. Compared with its peak of $162 billion in 1987, the US current account deficit dropped more than 30 percent by 1989; yet it was still above the 1984 level of $99 billion. Similarly, by 1989 the Japanese current account surplus had dropped 34 percent from its peak in 1987. The German surplus, on the other hand, increased 22 percent during the 1987–89 period; however, this development did not become much of a political issue between the United States and Germany, because most of the surplus was run with other European countries.

The data in tables 4.5 and 4.6 are in terms of nominal balances; the G-7 participants chose to concentrate on these because of the political significance accorded them, particularly in the United States. Measured as a share of GNP, however, the trends in these balances showed greater progress: the US current account deficit dropped to 2.1 percent of GNP in 1989 from its peak of 3.6 percent in 1987; the Japanese surplus dropped to 2.0 percent in 1989 from its peak of 4.4 percent in 1986; the German surplus, however, after falling in 1987 from its 1986 peak of 4.4 percent, climbed to 4.6 percent in 1989.

In 1990 and 1991, with corresponding changes occurring in net private capital flows and reserves of monetary authorities, the trends in Japan and the United States are expected to continue. The US deficit is projected by the IMF to continue dropping to 1.7 percent of GNP in 1991. Japan's surplus was projected to stabilize in the 1.8 percent range in 1990 and 1991. Germany's surplus is projected to drop to 2.3 percent of GNP in 1991 as national savings are redirected toward domestic investment with reunification (International Monetary Fund 1990, table A31, 144).

The principal concern that large current account imbalances raise is whether they are "sustainable." Sustainability is gauged with respect to both external and internal factors. External sustainability is determined by whether the imbalance is compatible with "normal" net capital flows. Economists' views on this question vary. Frenkel and Goldstein (1986) have pointed out the difficulties involved in specifying whether the United States is "normally" a net capital exporter or importer, given the instability of perceived investment opportunities across countries.

Bergsten (1988) emphasizes internal sustainability in assessing the significance of current account imbalances. In particular, he relates massive imbalances to the emergence of destabilizing protectionist pressures like those that built up in the United States in the 1980s. Bergsten has also argued that the constant threat of financial and economic instability posed by huge current account deficits—and the resulting need to attract capital inflows—undermines the international leadership position of the United States. In 1988, he prescribed a goal of eliminating the deficit in the first term of the new US president—thus striking a balance between those economists who believe that the United States should run current account surpluses to restore confidence in the dollar, and those who think it can prudently run a modest deficit while aiming to stabilize the relationship between net foreign debt and GNP.

Changing Output and Domestic Demand Differentials

Another goal of policy coordination was to change output and domestic demand differentials among the major countries, to reduce external imbalances and at the same time sustain world growth. To contribute to this goal, surplus countries were expected to increase the growth of their domestic demand, both to absorb production that might otherwise be exported and to stimulate imports. The deficit countries were expected to dampen domestic demand to allow expenditure switching to occur between tradeables and nontradeables, and to take pressure off domestic interest rates.

The record, summarized in table 5.8, shows partial success. Real domestic demand growth in the United States slowed to less than 2 percent in 1989; output growth began to outpace that of domestic demand in 1987. In Japan, meanwhile, domestic demand surged from 4 percent in 1985 to nearly 6 percent in 1989, while the rate of output growth dropped increasingly far behind. In Germany, domestic demand increased from its near-stagnant level of 1985, but the rate of output growth, after dropping below that of domestic demand in 1987, doubled from 1987 to 1989.

Realigning and Stabilizing the Dollar

The record points to success in realigning and stabilizing the dollar (both in nominal terms, as shown in figure 5.2, and in real terms) within a range since late 1987. In nominal terms, the dollar hit a low of DM1.59 in the first week of 1988, and then varied (until the second half of 1990) between its December 1987 level and a peak of nearly DM2.00 in mid-1989. Against the yen, the dollar has followed a different pattern, reaching a low of ¥123 in the first week of 1988, and moving into the range of ¥144 to ¥157 in the first half of 1990.

TABLE 5.8 Real growth in domestic demand and output in the G-7 countries, 1985–89 (percentages per year)

Country	1985		1987		1989	
	Domestic demand	Output	Domestic demand	Output	Domestic demand	Output
Canada	5.3	4.8	5.2	4.0	4.1	3.0
Japan	4.0	4.9	5.4	4.6	5.9	4.9
United States	3.8	3.4	3.0	3.4	1.9	2.5
France	2.5	1.9	3.3	2.2	3.1	3.6
Germany	0.8	1.9	3.3	1.6	3.1	3.9
Italy	2.7	2.6	4.7	3.0	3.3	3.2
United Kingdom	2.8	3.7	5.5	4.7	3.1	2.2

Source: Organization for Economic Cooperation and Development, *OECD Economic Outlook*, various issues.

In the second half of 1990, the dollar depreciated against both currencies: in real effective terms the US currency fell to its lowest level in at least 30 years. The decline in the dollar has reflected a significant narrowing in interest rate differentials and strong cyclical growth in Japan and Germany at a time when US growth has slowed significantly.

Here again, as with current account balances, the important question is whether the range within which the key currencies have moved since early 1988 is consistent with medium-term equilibrium. Economists differ on this issue; the conclusions they arrive at depend in part on the methodology employed to estimate equilibria. One method is based on the concept of purchasing power parity: in this view, the equilibrium nominal exchange rate is that which aligns national price levels of internationally traded goods, as measured by producer or wholesale price indexes (see McKinnon 1988, 83–104, and the comments by Dornbusch and Williamson accompanying that article). A competing method holds that the equilibrium exchange rate is that rate consistent with internal macroeconomic balance and a sustainable current account balance in the medium term (see Williamson 1985).

The practical issue, however, is whether the level of the exchange rate is consistent with the direction of underlying policies—in the 1980s this has meant in particular the US fiscal stance. The further slowdown of US domestic demand growth in 1990 and credible measures legislated in the autumn of that year to reduce the US budget deficit are consistent with a lower dollar. A related question is whether the authorities were successful in stabilizing the key currencies within agreed ranges. This issue is dealt with in the next section, where it is shown that policy coordination was successful only at times—and for good reason.

THE CONTRIBUTION OF POLICY COORDINATION

The accomplishments of the policy coordination process can be assessed with respect to the key elements of the process: the analytical framework, the policy guidelines set, and policy implementation. The first two elements were the subject of the previous chapter. The focus in this section is on the extent to which the coordination process can be credited with influencing desired policy changes, particularly changing differentials between output and domestic demand growth, changing fiscal policies in surplus and deficit countries, realigning and then stabilizing the dollar, and promoting structural reforms.

Such an action-oriented focus would be incomplete by itself, however; there have been other important outcomes of the coordination discussions, such as changes in ministers' and officials' attitudes and in their perceptions of spillovers, reductions in international frictions, and the heading off of crises. The impact of policy coordination, therefore, is evaluated in two ways: in terms of what did happen and in terms of what did not.

What Did Happen

There is evidence that coordination had a direct impact on national policies, either through the exertion of peer pressure or as a result of commitment to what participants saw as mutually beneficial policy changes. The evidence is clearest in 1987 when, at the Louvre meeting and thereafter, a package of policy changes widely regarded as necessary to reduce external imbalances was committed to and largely implemented by the G-7 (the US and German parts of the package did not materialize until after the October stock market crisis of that year). The evidence presented in this chapter also indicates that concerted intervention plus policy changes played a role in realigning and stabilizing the dollar (although these changes were already under way).

Another change that can be attributed to the policy coordination process was an increased awareness among treasury ministers of the need for greater discipline in the conduct of macroeconomic policy. Because of the prevalence of domestic protectionist pressures throughout the period, the process also contributed to an awareness of the desirability of a policy climate that favored open markets and greater economic flexibility through structural reform.

A third success, due more to coordination among central banks than among treasuries, was the generalized tightening of monetary policy in the 1988–89 period, when growth was stronger than expected and inflationary pressures began to emerge in some countries. Treasuries in those countries experiencing particularly strong inflationary pressures supported this generalized tightening and cautioned their less-troubled colleagues to do so as well—which they did. This episode can be cited as one in which countries pursued what Marris (see chapter 1) calls the "global objective": the participants viewed containing inflationary pressures as necessary to meet a common goal rather than as satisfying their individual ones.

Disentangling the impact of coordination from other influences on internal and external macroeconomic policy is more difficult. The impact of the coordination process on fiscal policy in the 1980s is mixed. The main lesson to be drawn is that, although virtually all of the requisite fiscal policy changes were already in train for reasons of good domestic policy, coordination broadened their scope and accelerated their timing. (Analysts of the Bonn Summit in 1978 found similar effects from that effort at policy coordination.)

International negotiations played a role in bringing external pressure to bear on Japanese fiscal policy in 1987, with the result that the Japanese government slowed the rate at which fiscal stimulus was withdrawn (table 5.4). In this case, although Japanese policymakers had discussed the need for greater stimulus since the yen had begun to strengthen in 1985, external pressure speeded the final decision, and the prospect of taking political credit at the Venice Summit even prompted Prime Minister Nakasone to top up the package. Two other internal factors played a role in the decision: the availability of funds for stimulus, resulting from privatization of some of the assets of Japan National Railways and the sale of NTT (the Japanese telecommunications conglomerate); and widespread public support for policy changes in order to maintain "smoothness in international relations."

In Germany, external pressure for fiscal stimulus was largely resisted; but the need to respond in a coordinated way to the October 1987 crisis played a role in the German decision in December to increase the commitment to structural reform. Two other countries with large fiscal deficits, Canada and Italy, were careful to limit their deficit reduction commitments to what they felt was politically feasible at home.

One of the weaknesses of the coordination process is the apparent asymmetry in the degree to which the G-7 countries can effectively exert peer pressure on each other. The US administration is far less amenable to pressure for fiscal policy changes than are other governments, and indeed the other participants have refrained from applying such pressure because they were skeptical about its impact. In the United States itself, coordination is widely seen as having little impact. Yet the commitments made by Congress and the administration at their 1987 budget summit were at least in part a response to pressures from other governments, as well as from domestic sources, the media, and the financial markets.

One way to disentangle the effects of coordination from other influences is to pose the counterfactual case of what might have happened in the absence of coordination. On the matter of reducing current account imbalances, the distinction has been made in official circles between policy-induced and market-induced adjustment; without the coordination process (and policy-induced adjustment), adjustment would have been faster, but more disruptive, because markets would have forced it. The US administration and Congress would have had to face up to the fiscal problem sooner, since it would not have had the burden-sharing argument with Japan and Germany to hide behind (as Martin Feldstein [1988a, 11] has argued).

Perhaps. But coordination did head off some major costs of sudden adjustment that a market crisis would have imposed. It is likely that such a crisis would indeed have occurred in the absence of coordination, and it surely would have been disruptive and costly in terms of undermining economic confidence. Through the coordination process, the inevitable consequences of persisting in bad fiscal policy were repeatedly brought to the awareness of the US administration. Moreover, as needed policy changes occurred in the other major countries, the onus for action shifted by default to the United States.

The counterfactual approach also provides some insights into the role of coordination in the 1987 stock market crash. The runup in stock prices in 1987 had created a speculative bubble that was certain to burst sooner or later; if the uncertainties created by public G-7 disagreement over economic policy had not precipitated the collapse, some other factor, such as the further bad news on the US trade deficit that came later in the autumn, would have. The risk in 1987 was that, in the absence of close G-7 cooperation, the financial crisis could have turned into an economic crisis. Had the authorities turned their backs and refused to cooperate among themselves, it is very likely that the crisis would have deepened. The package of policy changes and concerted foreign-exchange intervention might eventually have occurred piecemeal, but not without extensive disruption first. It should be noted, however, that lines of communication among central banks worked well in handling the liquidity implications of the stock market collapse, and would have done so even in the absence of intergovernmental coordination.

What Did Not Happen

Although the G-7 succeeded in realigning and then stabilizing the dollar for a period of time, it continued to fluctuate in a fairly wide range. Reference ranges remained ad hoc and came to be perceived as determined more by markets than by governments. Official views differed as to whether exchange rate stability was properly an objective of coordination, or whether the exchange rate was to be managed as an instrument of adjustment. Each approach, properly defined, involves taking some view of the macroeconomic state of the world and dealing with national imbalances through changes in macroeconomic policies. Each also requires acknowledgment that currency markets are not fully rational, and that there will be occasions when intervention, possibly accompanied by changes in monetary policy, may be necessary. Each approach requires participants to take a stand about what is the sensible level for the exchange rate in light of the fundamentals. This the G-7 participants had begun to do by mid-1989.

Another policy area in which the coordination process had less impact than intended was in incorporating microeconomic policy reform into the surveillance process. The main obstacle here was the jurisdictional problem (described in the section on "Microeconomic Policy" above). These constraints have since been overcome, but in ways that suggest that the issues are better handled outside of the G-7 coordination process. First, bilateral problems between Japan and the United States were taken up in the Structural Impediments Initiative (SII) talks initiated in mid-1989.[9] Second, the OECD, which has been working on structural issues since the late 1970s, began in 1990 to formalize a review and appraisal process. A progress report on structural reform was made public as a supplement to the June 1990 *OECD Economic Outlook*; the report summarizes the policy changes that member governments have undertaken or are committed to, and prescribes further changes. Finally, structural reform has also become a subject for routine review in the context of the OECD's annual peer reviews of country performance and prospects.

Some of the most valuable contributions of the coordination process also lie in what did not happen but could have. For example, coordination played a role in averting a protectionist wave in the US Congress in 1985. The Plaza Agreement and the concerted foreign-exchange intervention that followed were, at a minimum, a factor in dampening these protectionist pressures. Although some, pointing out that the rate of decline in the US dollar did not change after the Plaza, question whether intervention had any

---

9. The first phase of the SII talks was brought to a conclusion at the end of June 1990, when a joint report to President Bush and Prime Minister Kaifu was issued in which each country committed itself publicly to undertake a number of measures designed to improve the efficiency of its economy over a five-year period. (See US Treasury 1990.)

dollar did not change after the Plaza, question whether intervention had any real impact, others (e.g., Loehnis 1989) recall that sentiment before the Plaza meeting about the prospects for continued dollar decline was not very hopeful.

Coordination also probably averted a more serious economic crisis in 1987, in the wake of the global stock market collapse. Another aspect of the G-7's successful preventive maintenance has been its participants' consistent joint emphasis on the need to keep their markets open to international trade. This has contributed to a climate among treasury ministers that supports this broader objective, and may have played a role in preventing the emergence of stronger protectionist policies during the period.

Major pitfalls of coordination were also avoided: governments did not coordinate the wrong policies; coordination contributed, as argued earlier, to policy changes that moved in the right direction to reduce external imbalances and contribute to dollar stability (although average inflation was rising by the end of the period).

Finally, governments did not engage in beggar-thy-neighbor policy changes, such as competitive depreciations (although there were some fears of competitive interest rate increases in 1987). Nor did they synchronize policy changes, such as occurred in 1981, when most major central banks tightened monetary policy simultaneously. Instead, policy changes were largely complementary, as was the intent of the coordination process.

6   The Past as Prologue

Does the performance of the G-5 and G-7 from 1985 to 1989 suggest that it is time for a requiem for economic policy coordination? Or have we heard only the prologue? If the latter, what changes are needed to make coordination work more effectively? The answers to these questions have dimensions of both substance and process.

The generally improved performance of the major industrialized economies in the latter half of the 1980s supports the thesis that coordination made a positive *substantive* contribution. Economic problems that had built up in the first half of the decade began to unwind. Current account imbalances declined. The US fiscal deficit dropped to less than 3 percent of GNP in 1989 from nearly 5 percent in 1987. US domestic demand growth slowed while Japanese domestic demand boomed and even German domestic demand picked up from near stagnant levels. The dollar fell against the deutsche mark and the yen and stabilized in a lower range after the end of 1987.[1] The feared hard landing of the US economy was avoided.

These developments were not the result of mere luck. Cooperation among governments to change policies and to manage needed adjustments in exchange rates played a role. Just how much credit the G-7 process can take for the policy changes that occurred and the improved performance that was observed is impossible to quantify precisely. The impact of coordination must be disentangled from what would have happened anyway.

---

1. By late 1990, the dollar had reached historic lows against the mark and had weakened sharply against the yen. Narrower interest rate differentials, reflecting strong domestic demand growth in Germany and Japan and the slowdown in US economic activity, contributed to the weaker dollar. Uncertainty surrounding the outcome of the Persian Gulf crisis and the decision to further reduce the federal budget deficit in October were also contributing factors. The effects of the US recession, the weaker dollar, and the need to rebuild the former East Germany and for internal restructuring in Japan speeded up the external adjustment process beyond what even the optimists had hoped could be achieved by policy coordination alone.

The most immediate evidence of the effect of concerted action appeared in the foreign-exchange markets. Intervention by the G-7 treasuries and central banks was successful at times in signaling their intention to change policies. Yet even as they carried out their commitments, the monetary authorities became increasingly wary of a tendency to use concerted intervention as a substitute for necessary changes in other policies. Political constraints continued to slow the implementation of the structural reforms and fiscal policy changes ultimately required to reduce international imbalances.

It is difficult to discern to what extent governments took actions, either because of their enhanced awareness of interdependence or in response to external pressure, that they might not otherwise have taken. The clearest evidence of such influence is seen in Japan, where *gaiatsu* (foreign pressure) was a major factor in the 1985–87 period in inducing the government to increase public works spending.[2] *Gaiatsu* was also important to the success of the Structural Impediments Initiative (SII) talks in 1990.

There is evidence that G-7 pressure has been used as a policy lever in the United States as well: in 1989, Treasury Secretary Nicholas F. Brady publicly cited pressure from his G-7 colleagues as an argument to persuade Congress to agree to the Bush administration's deficit reduction proposals. In all these instances, the policy changes being sought were already under active discussion domestically, on their own domestic merits. Peer pressure was used in these cases to nudge things along.

The record of the G-5 and G-7 in constructing for themselves a workable *process* of policy coordination is a mixed one: after a promising start in 1985–87, the coordination process deteriorated in 1988 and 1989. Even in the earlier period, coordination occurred in more or less sporadic bursts, months or even years apart—the Plaza Agreement in 1985, the Louvre Accord in February 1987, the December 1987 "telephone accord"—rather than as a continuous process. Cooperation was even looser during 1988 and 1989. Agreement had been reached on the overall goals of the process and what was needed to achieve them, but a sense of inertia with respect to implementation was perceived to have set in. No new package agreements emerged. The surveillance process became systematized, but the G-7 members found

---

2. Funabashi (1989, 104–07) recounts the internal battles in the Japanese government that led to a compromise between the "domesticists" defending fiscal austerity and the "internationalists" pushing for US cooperation in currency realignment.

it difficult to fulfill their fiscal policy commitments and to agree on intervention tactics.

Several reasons account for this apparent deterioration of the process. First, surveillance discussions lost their initial crispness as the slow implementation of policy commitments shifted the dialogue to repetitive discussions of remedial action. Second, the urgency of the imbalances problem had faded by the end of the decade in the absence of further crises after 1987, introducing a sense of complacency. Third, the almost-complete turnover of treasury ministers that occurred between late 1988 and late 1989 contributed to a loss of momentum. It was also easy for the attention of the new players to become diverted to such issues as the role of the IMF and the World Bank in Third World debt strategy and the question of IMF quota enlargement. A fourth reason stemmed from the ad hoc nature of the surveillance process. The absence of a chairman, of any record of decisions, and of a permanent secretariat added to the difficulties of exerting peer pressure.

Cooperative discussions revealed differing views about the linkages between goals and instruments and a lack of agreement on the role of the exchange rate in the adjustment process. Some tended to see the exchange rate as an objective in itself (even though the agreed objective was to reduce external imbalances), while others saw it as an instrument. These differences made bargaining more difficult, with participants sometimes talking past each other.

Finally, a major factor contributing to the erosion of the process was the asymmetry in the degree of mutually exerted peer pressure. Although there was agreement that the burden of adjustment should be shared, US Treasury officials tended to try to shift the burden onto other participants, and to regard concerted foreign-exchange intervention as a substitute for policy change. This undermined the sense of mutual trust that is essential for successful cooperation. By early 1989, US deficit reduction was seen as central to reducing the imbalances that remained, yet the other participants failed to press the case hard with the new administration. One reason for this failure was their perception that the US representatives could not, by themselves, deliver. The US officials also succeeded in deflecting peer pressure by conveying an optimistic picture of the chances for a bipartisan deficit reduction agreement that would head off Gramm-Rudman-Hollings sequestration.

The overall verdict on the G-7 coordination process, with respect to both substance and process, is therefore mixed. Economic performance has by and large improved (the 1990–91 recession in the United States notwithstanding), and progress continues to be made on the underlying economic problems. But these problems are not yet resolved, and new ones can be seen on the horizon. Despite the October 1990 budget accord, the US fiscal deficit may rise again under the impacts of recession and the additional defense expenditures incurred in the Persian Gulf war. Current account imbalances are beginning to approach sustainable levels, but protectionism in the large industrial countries is still a systemic threat.[3] Demand for funds to rebuild Eastern Europe can be expected to increase. Combined with the already large claims of the OECD countries on world savings (the OPEC countries and the Asian newly industrializing countries will be the main funding sources), this means that, if renewed upward pressures on real interest rates are to be avoided in the medium term, the OECD governments should reduce their claims by running public-sector budget surpluses.

The process created to address these issues cooperatively, which now consists essentially of a surveillance framework and some accumulated (but ad hoc) experience with reference ranges, has not been protected against the intrusion of other issues, which, although urgent, are extraneous to the central task of policy coordination. Because of differing views among (and within) participating governments and the imperfect state of knowledge about the linkages between goals and instruments, the accomplishments of the 1985–89 period are less than they should have been. More could and should be done to promote agreement and to improve the knowledge foundation on which policy decisions can be based.

Yet if it is too soon to praise the G-7's achievements unreservedly, neither is the time come to bury the process. Since the G-5 reembarked on a serious cooperative approach to the problems of interdependence in 1985, they have been groping their way toward a new regime. To fail to protect it from being eroded as short-term issues monopolize officials' attention would be a shortsighted error, with potentially serious long-term consequences for the international monetary system. However, without an external crisis to rally support and attention, the G-7 process seems to be having its own internal

---

3. Indeed, at the time this manuscript went to press in early 1991, protectionism seemed to be a growing threat as negotiators in the suspended Uruguay Round of GATT talks encountered almost insurmountable obstacles to expanding market access to agricultural products and extending the reach of the GATT to address new forms of protectionism and trade in services.

identity crisis—something that often happens to organizations and individuals as they mature. All the more reason, then, to maintain the system in working order and strengthen it for the time, certain to come, when it will have to be relied upon, both to prevent crises and to manage them.

Five Criteria

From this perspective, the history of policy coordination in the 1985–89 period should be seen as a prologue. The relapse in the process since 1988 reveals major institutional shortcomings, but these can be overcome. One way to approach the question of how to improve the process is to imagine the G-7 countries starting afresh, *tabula rasa*, to create a new policy coordinating body: What key characteristics of the existing structures would they want to preserve, and what additional ones, lacking in the present arrangements, would they want to include? The analysis in the preceding chapters of this study suggests that among these key criteria would be the following: informality and frankness, a strong and clearly defined mandate, strong leadership and clear lines of accountability, an agreed-upon analytical framework with guidelines for remedial action, and a strong secretariat and technical support.

The first criterion, which ranks very high among the G-7 ministers and deputies, is that the coordinating body should conduct its affairs with *informality and frankness*. One of the features of the G-7 process most valued by its participants is the opportunity, unique in international meetings, to engage in frank exchange of information and views with one's counterparts. The same theme runs through the history of the economic summits, and is a principal reason why the summit leaders have resisted establishing a permanent supporting bureaucracy. National officials prefer to learn from and be influenced by each other, rather than by international civil servants.

There is an important tradeoff in international forums between informality and the close control it allows to the principal players, on the one hand, and the assurance of continuity formalization brings, on the other. Where meetings and exchanges are informal, officials feel sufficiently in control of events and believe they can identify and manage new problems efficiently and expeditiously as they arise. The introduction of formal procedures and a permanent staff in international institutions tends, on the other hand, to evolve into control by an ever-expanding secretariat and routinization of analysis and debate. Most official international bureaucracies have indeed expanded to take on lives and identities of their own, independent of their national constituencies. With the loss of a sense of control comes a decline in participants' willingness to be frank with each other. The insistence of the G-5 and G-7 on confidentiality in their relationships is directly related to the desire to preserve the frankness and informality that they have created for themselves.

A second criterion drawn from the recent G-7 experience is a *clearly defined mandate* for the group. It is true that the major countries have traditionally divided the issues on which they have conferred informally among themselves, for example into the differing mandates of the G-10 and WP3 described in chapter 2. However, the G-7 have allowed their agenda to become crowded in recent years with a hodgepodge of issues, to such an extent that the primary objectives of the policy coordination regime have received inadequate attention. The presence of these other issues may have preserved the cohesion of the group in difficult times when desired major policy changes, such as reduction of the US budget deficit, were slow in coming. Nevertheless, a more focused mandate is required along the lines of the framework applied in chapter 4: to monitor and assess global economic developments and prospects; to judge each other's performance against policy guidelines or standards; and to implement remedial policy action.

The third criterion is *strong leadership and clear lines of accountability*. Any group is more effective when it is well led and held strictly to account for carrying out its mandate. In both WP3 and the G-7 experience, satisfying this criterion depends on such factors as the personalities of the individual participants and the duration of their tenure; but more important are such factors as the mutuality of peer pressure exerted among the participants and a willingness to increase that pressure by raising issues to the top leadership level when necessary to ensure that remedial policies are carried out.

The fourth criterion is *an agreed-upon analytical framework and policy guidelines*. Lack of such a framework means that disagreements on remedial action will tend to be sustained and policy bargaining made more difficult. In the G-7 surveillance process, a set of selected economic indicators eventually became an accepted basis for objective assessment of the short-term economic outlook and derivative policy implications. But the present framework has its flaws (which are analyzed in detail in chapter 4): macroeconomic policy analysis becomes artificially separated from that of foreign-exchange market developments; the indicators chosen (in particular the use of nominal bilateral rather than real exchange rates) are in some cases rudimentary and misleading as guides to true economic relationships; conceptual and empirical analysis of the interactions between goals and instruments is underutilized. Little use has been made of principles or standards against which to judge alternative remedial policies.

A final criterion is to provide *an adequate secretariat and technical support,* to provide objective analysis of priorities and issues that should be on the group's agenda, and to ensure follow-through. Clearly, satisfying both this criterion and that of informality and frankness in the proceedings will be a challenge.

Five Proposals

These five criteria suggest certain specific actions that should be taken both to preserve what is valuable in the existing coordination structure and to develop it into a stronger and more effective one. The rest of this chapter develops five proposals for accomplishing this task. Ranked in order of importance, they are:

- Involve central bankers more closely;
- Integrate exchange rate and macroeconomic considerations in the surveillance process as well as in decision making;
- Create an institutional memory and support by building a better-defined professional base;
- Strengthen the methods for implementing remedial policies;
- Rationalize the process by reducing the number of participants.

1. INVOLVE CENTRAL BANKERS MORE CLOSELY

One of the most important ways to strengthen the existing framework would be to involve central bankers more closely in all policy coordination activities. As the analysis in the preceding three chapters has indicated, a recurrent weakness in both analysis and action has been the absence of central bank deputies from the G-7 process and the absence of central bank accountability for policy commitments made by the G-7.[4] Central bank governors attend ministerial meetings, but their deputies are not directly involved with treasury deputies in the preparations for those meetings. As a result, the treasuries play a disproportionate role in setting the G-7 agenda. Enhanced central bank involvement would help to integrate foreign-exchange market and monetary developments into the analytical framework (which is an issue distinct from the issue of coordinating monetary policy).

Central bankers should become more involved in all stages of the coordination process to reduce the ad hoc nature of the process and as part of the rationalization that will be required after stage II of European monetary union (EMU) has been achieved. Central bank deputies should be included in preministerial consultations and in the actual coordination discussions and decision-making meetings of the G-7.

The idea of involving central bank deputies is not new. The value of their participation has been demonstrated in the functioning of WP3. However, closer central bank participation in the G-7 process would have costs as well as benefits. The most important cost is one that the central bankers themselves have stressed, namely, the fact that their participation in analytical discussions would expose them more directly to pressures to coordinate monetary policies, which would diminish their independence in carrying out their primary responsibility. A second cost stems from the increased number of participants. G-5 veterans have expressed their surprise at how much the dynamics changed when Canada and Italy joined the group. They argue that adding seven more participants would reduce the informality and frankness of the discussions. A third cost arises from the fact that in some countries the central bank has little real independence from the treasury; inclusion of central bank deputies from such countries, rather than enrich the debate, might instead merely "pack" the G-7 with spokespersons for positions already represented.

---

4. Indeed, it could be argued that policy coordination might be turned over to the central banks by building it into the process under way at regular BIS meetings. Many of the central banks control most of the policy instruments that count. But because they are not directly accountable politically, this option is not the subject of serious consideration.

There are significant benefits to be gained, however, from the participation of central bank deputies. First, they would bring with them better information about monetary policy developments and increased sensitivity to conflicts between external and domestic objectives. The active presence of central bankers in the room would eliminate uncertainties in the other participants' minds about what, if any, policy changes the central banks are able and willing to deliver on—such uncertainties have hampered the process since the Louvre Accord. Because of the lags involved in using fiscal and structural policies, monetary policy has increasingly become the tool of choice for short-term policy action. Since central bankers are likely to be in on the landing, they should be in on the takeoff.

The second benefit of enhanced central bank participation is a paradoxical one. Because fiscal and structural policy changes are difficult to achieve politically, there is a tendency to rely on foreign-exchange intervention and monetary instruments, which are easier to manipulate. Central bankers can be expected to question this tendency and to press for consideration of the alternatives. Their participation could therefore help shift some of the burden of adjustment from monetary policy and exchange rates to fiscal and structural policy. Third, the special expertise of central bankers in certain areas of economic analysis would complement the economics skills of the treasury deputies, and thus deepen the substantive dialogue.

Until stage II of EMU is reached, the 14 treasury and central bank deputies should schedule regular surveillance sessions—say, twice a year.[5] This approach is unlikely, in the short term, to change much of what goes on outside the meetings, but it would build the basis for better analysis and understanding. After stage II of EMU, as defined in late 1990, the number of central banks involved would decline to four.

The central issue is one of building trust between independent central bankers and governments. Ideally, each country's treasury and central bank should be able to work together at home to produce policies that will sustain noninflationary economic growth. Recognizing the political limitations on achieving that ideal, this proposal addresses the need to rationalize the G-7 in a way that preserves the independence of the banks but recognizes the

---

5. Stage I of EMU, now in effect, involves the participation of all the EC countries in the exchange rate mechanism and liberalization of capital markets. The ECBS is to be set up in stage II, when commitments will also be made to fix exchange rates.

need for bank participation in the G-7's decisions in order for those decisions to be carried out.

2. INTEGRATE EXCHANGE RATE AND MACROECONOMIC CONSIDERATIONS

Surveillance will be improved by integrating exchange rate and macroeconomic considerations and by arriving at shared views of medium-term equilibrium exchange rate relationships.

The artificial separation of exchange rate from macroeconomic policy issues in the G-7's analytical framework is described in chapter 4 as one of the most serious weaknesses of the process. One reason why these considerations have not been integrated in the post–1987 surveillance process has been the fear, particularly on the part of Japan and Germany, that concerted intervention would be used to substitute for required macroeconomic policy changes.[6] This fear is not unfounded: in 1989, for example, further action on the US budget deficit would have been consistent with the objective of slowing the renewed rise of the dollar; however, such action was not forthcoming, and therefore intervention was used more intensely than the fundamentals would have suggested.

All participants have agreed in principle on the need at times for concerted intervention in foreign-exchange markets; none have been advocates either of benign neglect of free-floating exchange rates or of an immediate return to a system of fixed rates. Rather the debate has been one between "dirty fixers" and "dirty floaters." The dirty fixers seek clear-cut principles and rules to govern intervention tactics, but they do not question the need for intervention whenever significant misalignments occur (although it is not always clear whether they think it should be sterilized or unsterilized), even where the problem might be one of short-term volatility. Dirty floaters do not share this presumption; instead they are more concerned to consult about market conditions and economic fundamentals in order to develop a consensus, which might—or might not—lead to intervention.

The development of a shared understanding about the circumstances in

---

6. Although in 1986 US support for dollar stabilization was linked with Japanese commitments to stimulate growth of domestic demand.

which exchange rates should and should not move (as well as an improved understanding of the dynamics of currency markets and why they sometimes overshoot) could help to reconcile these differing tactical approaches. Such a reconciliation is essential to G-7 credibility in the markets, where it can provide an anchor to expectations either through public announcement of ranges for exchange rates or through the strenuous defense of confidential ranges.

The conduct of concerted intervention should change in several ways. Input to the discussion of equilibrium exchange rates in the surveillance process should be of the highest analytical quality and should come from an independent source such as the IMF. Concerted intervention should not be used as a substitute for policy changes when these are required, although it is possible to envisage the judicious use of coordinated interest rate changes along with concerted intervention to deal with a misalignment problem. Diagnosis of misalignment problems should be based on a shared assessment, and treatment on a joint agreement as to which policy instruments are appropriate to the problem. The shared assessment should also include a view of the macroeconomic state of the world as a whole, so that options can be considered in the light of how they will influence the collective goal of sustaining noninflationary world growth.

This approach does not preclude tighter exchange rate arrangements in the future that would more closely resemble target zones or ranges. Rather it is a realistic first step along that road, and one that should command wider support than the attempt to introduce the tight arrangements for reference ranges at the time of the Louvre Accord (discussed in chapter 4).

Economists have proposed various principles and rules for governments to follow in reducing current account imbalances and in stabilizing exchange rates. Bergsten (1988), for example, has called for the adoption of current account and fiscal targets by the United States. The blueprint published by Williamson and Miller (1987) suggests principles for demand management directed at both price stability and a limited countercyclical thrust.

Although the G-7 have from time to time used reference ranges for exchange rates, as proposed by Williamson and Miller, it is instructive to compare the gap between G-7 practice and blueprint theory. The authors of the blueprint propose that national authorities pursue two intermediate targets: the growth rate of domestic demand and a publicly announced zone for the real effective exchange rate. To achieve these targets, they propose three policy principles: use short-term deviations of national fiscal policy from a medium-term target consistent with the current account target to achieve the domestic demand growth target; use exchange market intervention, reinforced as necessary by short-term interest rate differentials, to maintain agreed-upon target zones for exchange rates; and stabilize growth of nominal world demand by varying world short-term interest rates.

Actual G-7 practice differs from these proposals in several respects:

- The biggest difference is in the measure of exchange rates used in surveillance. G-7 practice has been to use nominal rates; the possibility of adopting real rates or some measure of equilibrium exchange rates has been informally considered from time to time but has elicited little support, since these are not the rates used for management.
- The G-7 has not adopted formal targets. To pursue the objective of reducing imbalances, authorities have agreed to focus on changes in patterns of output and domestic demand, but they have not agreed to set targets for these variables. Reference ranges, which were used but never publicly acknowledged, bear some similarity to the target zone concept. However, differences of view about the operational significance of reference ranges were such that efforts to pursue a more ambitious concept such as target zones would have endangered the continued existence of the coordination process.
- External objectives for monetary policy, such as exchange rate stability, have not been explicitly accepted.
- Use of national fiscal policies by the G-7 as instruments for reducing current account imbalances have encountered obstacles in the national authorities' abilities and willingness to deliver on their commitments.

In short, differences of view about the role of exchange rates in the adjustment process and uncertainty about causal relationships account for the present gap between theory and practice. In view of these factors and the participants' resistance to greater formalization of the process, the immediate chances of adoption of policy rules of the rigor and formality of the blueprint are small.

3. CREATE AN INSTITUTIONAL MEMORY

The informality of G-7 coordination so highly valued by its participants is also a source of weakness. There is no formal chairman who decides what is to be done, by whom, and when. Issues needing discussion are identified informally; there is little preparation of objective analysis on which consideration of policy options can be based. Analytical and logistical support is provided on an ad hoc basis from individual treasuries and the IMF. Nor is there any objective observer or secretary to identify and record areas of agreement and disagreement in the discussions or in the group's decisions. The only shared record consists of the communiqués made public after the group's meetings.

There should be created an institutional memory and a support mechanism for the policy coordination process, in the form of an independent secretariat. The secretariat should work in confidence but be linked closely to the independent representative—currently the Managing Director of the IMF—participating in the ministerial meetings.

The current ad hoc structure of the G-7's deliberations derives from the informal, "anti-organizational" (to use the term employed by Putnam and Bayne 1987, 166) structure of the economic summits. As Putnam and Bayne note, summit leaders have traditionally limited themselves to endorsing or directing new initiatives rather than engaging in close bargaining. However, since the function of the G-7 is precisely to engage in analysis and negotiation, as well as decision making, it requires strong leadership and more technical and organizational support to carry out its tasks.

The present ad hoc approach has several undesirable consequences. First, it makes the coordination process vulnerable to discontinuity and instability as the individual participants change (which they do frequently, as we have seen in chapter 3). Funabashi (1989) has described the close working relationships that developed between US Treasury Secretary James Baker and his Japanese and German counterparts Kiichi Miyazawa and Gerhard Stoltenberg during the 1985–88 period; much of whatever utility derived from these relationships was inevitably lost after Baker's and later Miyazawa's departure. Similarly, continuity (and counterpoint) was provided by deputies David Mulford of the United States and Hans Tietmeyer of Germany during the same period.

When key participants change, the process can suffer because the departing members take with them part of its institutional memory, both of the rationale for coordination and of the details of its operation. This is particularly true with respect to the three large countries, whose ministers must provide continuity of vision and leadership, and whose deputies are the anchors for the work program and engage in much of the policy bargaining.

A senior European official has observed that treasury ministers, when they first acquire the portfolio, need a period of time to master the domestic fiscal and financial issues that are their primary responsibilities. Only when they are familiar with these are they in a position to turn to international issues.[7] Some newcomers are also seen to pass through a phase of skepticism about the importance of "all those international talkfests," where policy initiatives seem to move at a glacial pace. These attitudes usually change with experience, but they illustrate the variability in commitment to which an already ad hoc process can fall prey.

A second drawback to the ad hoc nature of the process is that it makes it nearly impossible to establish a sound analytical framework; the absence of such a framework was identified in chapter 4 as a principal weakness of the G-7 process. Without a permanent secretariat, there is no systematic way to identify issues and organize analysis so as to inform the participants' judgment of policy implications and options.

Third, without an objective referee, the agenda can easily be captured by short-term, often political, concerns. In 1989, for example, extensive discussion of a new Third World debt strategy crowded out macroeconomic surveillance for many months (see chapter 4). It was not until the dollar began to rise strongly, and questions began to be raised in public about G-7 indifference, that these issues regained a place on the agenda. An objective referee would be better placed than individual participants to ensure timely and regular attention to surveillance.

Fourth, since there is no objective record of the proceedings apart from the published communiqués, decisions are always open to *ex post* reinterpretation.

The first of these shortcomings might be addressed in part by greater involvement of central bankers, since they serve longer terms than their treasury counterparts. But a chair and a secretariat are also required. At present, the country hosting a G-7 meeting also acts as the chair. This means that a small subgroup usually performs the role on an ad hoc basis. To

---

7. See Bergsten (1986) for a chart depicting the fluctuations in US participation in management of the world economy in the 1960–86 period. The chart clearly shows how US involvement has tended to decline in the years immediately following a change in administration.

provide more continuity while retaining informality, the chair could be rotated among the treasury ministers of the United States, Japan, and Germany (or the European Community if and when European treasury functions become centralized) for a set term—say, three years—as has been the practice in the Committee of EC Central Bank Governors.[8]

Regarding formation of a secretariat, two options should be considered. One option is for the G-7 to create and recruit its own secretariat. This could be free-standing and independent. It should be small and consist of professionals with both practical and academic credentials, who are allowed to provide independent inputs (as opposed to reflecting particular national political or ideological perspectives). These individuals could be recruited from the private sector and universities as well as from the treasuries and central banks. The secretariat to the Committee of Twenty in the 1970s was an independent group of outstanding individuals seconded by the institutions with which they were affiliated; the secretariat provided to the EC Central Bank Governors operates in the same way.

In the past, secretariats have tended to be drawn from existing institutions (the G-10 secretariat, for example, is drawn from the IMF, the OECD, and the BIS); the precedent at the economic summits has been to delegate specific issues to task forces, which countries operate themselves and to which they provide voluntary support. In addition, the range of issues undertaken by the G-7 in recent years suggests that the secretariat is unlikely to remain small, unless its mandate is confined to macroeconomic and exchange rate issues, with other matters addressed in ad hoc task forces as they are now.

The second and recommended option is to make fuller use of the IMF. It is the logical candidate to fulfill the analytical and secretariat functions regarding macroeconomic and exchange rate issues. Indeed, the IMF is already obliged by its shareholders to practice surveillance of each other's exchange rate policies. The logic of using the IMF as a source for secretariat functions is evident to most G-7 participants, but some have fears that the high level of confidentiality needed to conclude exchange rate understandings would be undermined (IMF representatives are presently excluded from such discussions), and the idea runs counter to the preference to avoid institutionalizing the coordination mechanism. In addition, there are reservations about

---

8. This idea was suggested by C. Fred Bergsten.

using the IMF as a secretariat when institutional issues such as IMF quota review, for example, could create a conflict of interest. Yet the IMF staff's track record on preserving the informality, frankness, and confidentialty of G-7 macroeconomic policy coordination has been impeccable.

To protect the policy coordination process from being distracted by important but peripheral issues, governments should continue to organize ad hoc task forces, as it has from time to time in recent years, to deal with such issues. The IMF research staff is quite capable of organizing and improving the technical analysis available to the G-7 for these purposes. One analytical input in which some long-term investment is advisable is work on linkages between goals and instruments within and across economies. A number of the treasuries, most of the central banks, and the IMF now have their own multicountry macroeconometric models, or have access to one. These models are among the few vehicles available for assessing the linkages among economies in an internally consistent manner. Few ministers or deputies are enthusiastic about this kind of work. They tend to distrust quantitative sophistication of this kind, even as an aid to judgment, preferring to rely on their accumulated experience and back-of-the-envelope knowledge about linkages. But this kind of work is needed to build a better shared technical understanding of the connections across economies, which eventually will feed upward into the deputies' briefings.

A standing working group of technical officials should be created and given a mandate to pursue a joint work program to develop a better understanding of the channels by which policies and economic activities in one economy affect others, and of the options for coordinating policy to reduce undesired spillovers. The working group should include analysts from central banks and private-sector research organizations as well.[9]

---

9. A core working group on which to build is that coordinated by economists at the Brookings Institution and involving 12 "participating models": those developed by Data Resources, Inc. (DRI), the Commission of the European Communities, and the Economic Planning Agency of Japan; the LINK system of country models headquartered at the University of Pennsylvania; the University of Liverpool model; the Multicountry Model (MCM) developed by staff of the US Federal Reserve; the MINIMOD model developed at the IMF; the McKibbin-Sachs Global Simulation Model; the INTERLINK model developed at the Organization for Economic Cooperation and Development; the model developed by John Taylor and associates at Stanford University; the Wharton Econometrics Forecasting Associates' model; and the model developed jointly by the University of Minnesota and the Federal Reserve Bank of Minneapolis.

4. STRENGTHEN IMPLEMENTATION

To strengthen accountability and the implementation of policy commitments, changes are needed in the links between the G-7 coordination process and the annual economic summits. Changes are also needed in some national decision-making structures. Deputies' administrative responsibilities should be restructured in some countries in the interest of congruence between their G-7 mandates and their actual authority.

The G-7's successes in bringing about remedial policy action have occurred mainly in times of crisis and in response to market pressures. Peer pressure has been the main method of promoting policy action and has been exerted mainly among the three largest countries. No matter how strong this pressure might be, however, such obstacles as lack of involvement by top leaders, diffused domestic decision-making mechanisms, and diffused official responsibilities can frustrate its intent. Such frustration can lead to the use of other routes for exerting pressure, such as the US–Japan SII talks, to pursue policy commitments.

As we saw in chapter 3, the heads of the G-7 governments have largely turned the policy coordination process over to their treasury ministries and central banks. Especially in recent years the leaders have used the annual economic summits to address other than economic issues, such as the anti–drug trafficking offensive and global environmental issues. Although these are indeed vital concerns that call for concerted action at the highest level, the leaders also need to reemphasize their involvement in macroeconomic issues, to provide an additional accountability mechanism for the coordination process and to improve policy implementation.

National leaders are in a position to bargain among themselves across widely differing issues in a way that even their ministers cannot. In 1989, for example, an opportunity was missed to link changes in the Third World debt strategy, desired by the United States, to the goal of further change in US fiscal policy: the other participants were too pessimistic about the ability of the US government to make and deliver fiscal policy commitments, and therefore they failed to exert the necessary pressure. The importance of a commitment to reduce the US budget deficit could have merited its being raised to the summit level for direct consideration by the President and the other heads of government.

Other extenuating circumstances also partly explain why the issue did not receive further attention at the 1989 summit. One of these was the desire of the French summit hosts to preserve the harmony of the event, which coincided with the bicentenary of the French Revolution. The Paris Summit indicates a disturbing tendency to cosmetize the economic summits, as the leaders have increasingly put aside substantive but politically contentious issues to provide a better opportunity to "make each other look good." This implicit objective has tended in recent years to discourage ministers from raising major policy differences to the attention of the summit leaders. The leaders' rationale for delegating surveillance to the G-7 ministers and deputies in 1986 was to inject political clout into the process, yet that clout is being used less and less frequently to encourage the remedial policy actions necessary to the management of economic interdependence.

The importance the Japanese people attach to the summit process provides another means of using the summits to reinforce the G-7's efforts. The summit is one of the few major international institutions of which Japan was a founder; others such as the IMF and the OECD were founded before Japan became a member. Therefore the performance of the Japanese Prime Minister at the annual summit is a matter of great public interest and pride in Japan. This could afford the Prime Minister the opportunity to use the summit to address issues that cross jurisdictional boundaries, such as structural reform, in a way that would command wide political support within Japan.

In Japan, structural issues are the responsibility of the Economic Planning Agency, the Ministry of International Trade and Industry (MITI), the postal and telecommunications ministry, and other ministries besides the Ministry of Finance; structural reform therefore becomes very difficult to tackle among ministers of different countries acting on their own. If the Prime Minister so decided, summit preparation could become an important vehicle for reaching a policy bargain that crosses these jurisdictional boundaries. Indeed, the Japanese fiscal package in 1987, one of the successes of the coordination process, was accelerated through the political and bureaucratic system, and in the final days before the Venice Summit was actually increased by the Prime Minister.

Diffusion of decision-making responsibility among various national agencies has been a stumbling block to coordination. In the United States this has been true particularly with respect to fiscal deficit reduction; here the need for Congress to ratify executive commitments has been a major impediment to progress. Destler and Henning (1989) recommended the development of a "fast track" legislative procedure for fiscal policy commitments made at international meetings analogous to that used since 1974 to ratify international trade agreements: "Congress would commit itself in advance to an up-or-down vote, within 90 days, on a presidential proposal to implement a US fiscal policy commitment made at a G-5 or G-7 summit meeting."[10] As with trade packages, the exercise of this authority would require an increase in congressional involvement in shaping the package and the domestic implementing legislation.

There are also administrative obstacles to policy implementation. Policy coordination is a serious and complex business, and much of the work is in fact done by deputies. The personal characteristics of the principals are a not-inconsiderable factor in the chances of coordination's success. These characteristics should include:

- Demonstrated diplomatic skills;
- Experience with, and a sense of the workings and concerns of, financial markets;
- International economic experience in the public or the private sector;
- A background in economics.

In chapter 3 it was observed that the majority of G-7 deputies combine their international responsibilities with those for financial affairs. Few are economists, and few have responsibilities on the domestic side, or for broader economic strategy. These arrangements mean that few deputies are responsible for the macroeconomic policies they must monitor and negotiate, although they do have more responsibility for exchange rate policy (and some for intervention). Because of the difficulties they face in delivering policy changes, deputies' preferences may be biased in favor of intervention. In addition, fiscal policy changes usually are politically constrained, requiring legislation to implement, which implies that ministers may also have biased preferences for intervention. The potentially cumbersome implications of fiscal and monetary policy arrangements resulting from EMU reinforce these concerns.

---

10. Destler and Henning (1989, 163). They point out that the implementing legislation could be very broad to cover, within statutory limits, those instruments required to deliver on the President's international budgetary commitments—including changes in spending and taxation as well as laws governing entitlements.

For these reasons, some thought should be given to rearranging the pattern of officials' responsibilities, particularly those of treasury deputies. Destler and Henning (1989, 163), in their study of internal coordination of US policy, have suggested that reponsibilities for both domestic and international monetary matters in the US Treasury be given to the Under Secretary for Monetary Affairs, as was the practice until the time of the Brady Treasury. (Indeed, this suggestion was included in the transition proposals for the incoming Bush administration, but the practice was not changed in spite of officials' advice.) Other countries (such as Japan, where the G-7 deputy tends to occupy a staff position) also need to achieve better alignment of deputies' authority and responsibilities with the issues they must address in the G-7 deliberations.

5. RATIONALIZE THE PROCESS

After stage II of EMU is reached, the G-7 should be rationalized into a G-3 (with representatives of the newly integrated Europe, Japan, and the United States) or a G4[11] (the above three plus Canada). Reduction in the number of participants will promote the efficiency of the coordination process, reduce the transaction costs of policy bargaining, and encourage remedial policy actions. The interests of nonmember countries affected by spillovers will have to be strongly represented through other consultation mechanisms and by an independent party who is credible to all participants.

This proposal is based on consideration of the direction of international economic events in the early 1990s. Policymakers in the United States, Japan, and Europe are already beginning to think in terms of a tripolar world, the implications of which Bergsten (1990) has begun to probe. The heretofore dominant position of the United States in the global economy is being challenged by countries in Europe and East Asia with higher economic and productivity growth rates. Europe is becoming increasingly attractive as

---

11. The European Commission in its 1990 study of the economic benefits and costs of EMU also assumes such rationalization to result in a G-4.

THE PAST AS PROLOGUE   151

a destination of foreign investment; Japan continues to supplant the United States as a leader of technological change and a major creditor. As Bergsten (1990) points out, these three powers are becoming ever more alike than different on such key measures as GNP, as well as in their openness to and dependence on international trade and finance. This rise of Europe and Japan toward coequal economic status with the United States means that the international economic dialogue is increasingly becoming a "trialogue" among these three powers.

The United States and Japan already have a well-established track record of finding ways to address their own bilateral issues. Most recently they have created, in the 1989–90 SII negotiations, a mechanism that addresses a set of mutual demands for policy changes intended to improve the functioning of each other's economy (although opinions may differ about the actual results of this mechanism to date). Some European officials have shown interest in trilateralizing this mechanism, since relationships between Europe and Japan are at present much less developed.

The catalyst for the new tripolar thinking, however, is events in Europe. An intergovernmental conference was convened in Rome in December 1990 to begin negotiation of EMU, one aspect of which will be the creation of a supranational authority for participating countries in the form of a European Central Bank System (ECBS). As this manuscript went to press, the EC governments intended that EMU arrangements should be negotiated to include all 12 members. But given divergent inflation rates and monetary policies within the group, it is possible that the arrangements will initially involve a smaller number of countries prepared to commit themselves to a single monetary and exchange rate policy. Political and institutional changes are under way as well. The growing commitment in Europe to economic, monetary, and political union foreshadows a global political and economic role for an integrated Europe.

Meanwhile Japan's growing economic power has created external expectations for greater Japanese leadership in international economic relations. The acknowledged role of hegemon played by the United States during the Cold War is fading as the security threat posed by the Soviet Union disappears. Increasingly in the years ahead we can expect joint leadership of the international trade and financial system by Europe, Japan, and the United States. The United States will still, for a time at least, be the leader, but more in the sense of a "managing partner" than as chief executive.

With this redistribution of global economic dominance, it is likely that the

G-7 will be replaced by a G-3 or (if Canada maintains its seat) a G-4, with a hierarchy of lesser relationships developed between them and the smaller economies. Such a rationalization through reduction in the number of players will reduce transaction costs, but also the number of differing views that get heard at the top level (Currie et al. 1989). Practical administrative arguments also support such a rationalization, since there are already too many international meetings and too many demands on the time of ministers.

To ensure broad support for such a rationalization, channels will have to be established for conveying information and differing views upward, as well as for reporting of discussions and decisions back downward.[12] Information could be supplied from (and reports made to) several well-established forums for surveillance and policy cooperation, particularly Article IV consultations within the IMF and discussions at the OECD in the Economic Policy Committee and its WP3. These forums have a stronger substantive basis than the G-7, thanks to the analytical input they receive from, and the direct involvement of, their highly professional secretariats. Whereas Article IV consultations take place on a bilateral basis between IMF staff and individual member countries, officials of other countries participate in detailed Executive Board discussions.[13] Similarly, WP3 is a valuable forum for discussion of the many issues affecting balance of payments, since it is the only forum in which central bank deputies also participate at present.

Rationalization of the G-7 process is not likely to occur in the next two or three years, for several reasons. First, the smaller G-7 members are likely to resist. They, after all, are the ones most affected by spillovers from policies

---

12. Bergsten et al. (1976), addressing the need for collective leadership in the international system, proposed a series of "concentric circles of decision-making," in which a core group of key countries involved in a particular issue would make decisions on a common course of action after consultations with closely associated countries. Once the core had reached agreement, each of the core members would seek to broaden the agreement through further discussions with its associates. Implementation would come through existing institutions, in which all relevant countries would become involved.

13. Article IV of the IMF Articles of Agreement require the IMF to maintain surveillance of members' exchange rate and economic policies and performance. The results of these regular reviews by IMF staff, including their policy recommendations, are discussed in confidence with national authorities. These results are also reviewed by the Executive Board of the IMF, which is responsible for conducting the Fund's business. All IMF members are represented on the Executive Board: the five largest members each appoint their own representative, whereas the remaining members are elected by constituencies of members.

adopted by the larger countries, and therefore they have the most to gain from pursuit of well-coordinated policies. They also play an important role as buffers and honest brokers, often returning the group's focus to substantive issues when discussion becomes constrained by political differences. The IMF cannot substitute for the smaller countries in this role; Germany, Japan, and the United States are all unwilling to cede to the IMF the requisite authority. Even if they did, the non–G-7 IMF members would also have to be persuaded to agree to such an exclusive role for IMF staff. The IMF's role is therefore likely to remain that of an ally to the G-7 process.

Second, the European countries have not yet decided whether they will cede political and fiscal authority to the European Parliament and the Economic Commission after stage II of EMU is reached. Unless and until they do, they will expect to participate in international discussions on fiscal and structural policy coordination. In a recent examination of the international implications of EMU, Alogoskoufis and Portes (1990) point out that EMU could reduce the difficulties of international fiscal policy coordination if it enables Europeans to speak with a more united voice on these issues than they did in the early 1980s and are therefore in a stronger bargaining position vis-à-vis the United States. The European Commission, in its 1990 study of the economic costs and benefits of EMU, assumes that fiscal policy authority will remain at the national level (Commission of the European Communities 1990, chapter 7).[14] Such decentralization is likely to be unwieldy, making international coordination more, not less, difficult. Failure to rationalize responsibility could mean that fiscal policy issues are not dealt with effectively in international discussions, with the result that monetary policy, which will be easier to coordinate under EMU, will bear still more of the burden of adjustment.

Some European officials suggest the G-7 should simply grow into a G-8, to include the ECBS, in order to reflect European allocations of responsibility. Alogoskoufis and Portes (1990) suggest a more workable alternative: continue the G-7 meetings as they are but with a reduced number of central bank governors (those of the G-3 plus the President of the ECBS). But as those authors point out, even this configuration is likely to exacerbate

---

14. This assumption is based on the principle of subsidiarity, by which economic policy functions remain at the national level unless they can be discharged more efficiently at the Community level.

existing dissatisfaction in the smaller European countries, which already feel excluded from the international coordination process. Since part of this opposition is to the prospect of having to live with a "directorium" of the four European members of the G-7 within EMU, continued pressures for rationalization of the G-7 can be expected.

A way should be found to designate one treasury minister to represent the Community in international discussions. This representative should have the authority to negotiate and deliver on commitments, and therefore should be chosen for a longer term than the six-month revolving presidency of the Community (say, three years—the term served by the chairman of the Committee of EC Central Bank Governors) and come from a country with major economic clout in the Community.

This subject is likely to be discussed for some time. National governments in Europe are unlikely to agree to tie their hands on the use of fiscal policy for domestic stabilization purposes at the same time that they do so on monetary policy. But they have been willing to commit to closer policy coordination at the ministerial level; if this commitment continues to grow, it should increase their ability to speak to third countries with one voice.

All members of the G-7 will have to reconsider the options available to them for building relationships in the emerging tripolar world. Germany, France, and Italy have already opted for more centralized European financial and economic relationships. As the dominant economy, Germany's role vis-à-vis the European Commission remains to be sorted out. The United Kingdom has entered the exchange rate mechanism, and Prime Minister John Major has signaled his intention to play a somewhat different political role than his predecessor in the negotiations on European political and economic union.

Canada poses a special case with regard to rationalization of the G-7. The case for including Canada on a par with the United States, Japan, and a united Europe is not strong given Canada's small economic size relative to these three. Yet the idea of allowing the United States to speak for Canada is anathema to most Canadians. Recent US presidents have tended to sympathize with Canadian sensitivities, recognizing Canada's past contributions to international security arrangements and its prominence in international trade.[15] But Canada's impact on the international financial system is not of

---

15. The "Quadrilateral" group of trade ministers representing Japan, the European Community, the United States, and Canada was created at the 1981 Ottawa Summit as part of the preparations for the 1982 ministerial meeting that launched the Uruguay Round of the General Agreement on

the same magnitude—although as a small, open economy with a flexible exchange rate, its interests in the structure and functioning of the system are considerable. It seems likely that the G-7 will not be replaced, at least for a time, by a G-4 or a G-3 until governments have sorted out these issues.

Implications for the International Monetary System

The lessons from the G-7 experience have implications for the future of the international monetary system. Policy coordination can be strengthened in the ways outlined above, but questions remain about the nature of the regime itself. Many hold the view that the international monetary system should be reformed not merely for the sake of reducing international trade and financial imbalances but to promote greater exchange rate stability as well.

In recent years, however, there has been no consensus among governments that problems in the international monetary system are serious enough to warrant further changes. The G-10 agreed to improved arrangements for surveillance (Group of Ten 1985), and the Plaza Agreement and Louvre Accord certainly did involve fundamental changes in the management of exchange rates. Yet in 1988, study within the G-7 of ways to improve the functioning of the international monetary system (described in chapter 4) produced an unusually opaque outcome, reflecting the absence of agreement among authorities on whether there was in fact a problem, and if so, what to do about it.

If governments decide in future to focus again on reforming the international monetary system, it will be important first of all to agree on the nature of the problem. At least two different goals might be envisaged: that of greater exchange rate stability, and that of ensuring that the authorities err on the side neither of inflation nor of deflation in pursuing growth objectives.

Although a recent survey (Edison and Melvin 1990) has concluded that the empirical evidence of the costs of exchange rate misalignments and volatility is insufficient for policy conclusions, proposals to address exchange

---

Tariffs and Trade (see Putnam and Bayne [1987, 131, 157] on the origins of the "Quad"). Canada has close trading ties with each of the G-3, which provides a rationale for its membership in this group.

rate instability have been offered. The advocates of target zones would set medium-term exchange rate targets compatible with sustainable current account balances and use short-run exchange rate management to keep the exchange rate within a wide band around the estimated sustainable levels. For reasons discussed in chapter 4, the proponents of target zones have been unable to overcome doubts among skeptics about the difficulties of defining sustainable levels, of agreeing to the frequent changes in nominal rates that might be required, or of providing a nominal anchor for the system.

If the problem with the international monetary system is considered more one of sustaining noninflationary global growth, the approach might be quite different. Frankel (forthcoming 1991a) has proposed international nominal targeting as a simplified framework that could overcome some of the main obstacles to macroeconomic policy coordination. He proposes one indicator—nominal domestic demand—for which national authorities would set targets each year, and a second—nominal GNP (domestic demand plus international balance on goods and services)—which would be targeted for the coming five years. Frankel would leave it to the national authorities to choose the instrument by which the nominal demand target is reached.

Agreement among governments on the nature of the problems to be addressed in any systemic reform would be a large step forward. There is a dearth not of proposals but of the will to consider them seriously. Little political pressure exists for further change in current global arrangements, although in Europe the decision to negotiate EMU was based on a far-reaching political vision. As the historical review in chapter 2 of this study indicated, substantive change in the international monetary system has usually occurred only in times of crisis.

Further evolution in the management of economic interdependence will require a great deal of committed leadership as well as major changes in attitude and mindset. Leaders and officials must think in terms of interdependence and the external consequences of domestic policies, as European governments have already been doing on a regional level, rather than simply try to avoid those consequences or to shift the burden elsewhere. A meaningful first step toward economic policy coordination at the global level was taken in the second half of the 1980s, but there has been backsliding since then. Governments can get the process back on track by taking the five steps proposed in this chapter. As a single world economy emerges, there will be no room for complacency in meeting the challenges of interdependence.

References

Alogoskoufis, George, and Richard Portes. 1990. "International Costs and Benefits from EMU." *Discussion Paper Series no. 424*. London: Centre for Economic Policy Research (June).

Bank of Japan. 1988. *Functions and Organization of the Bank of Japan*. Tokyo: Bank of Japan (March).

Balladur, Edouard. 1988. "Rebuilding an International Monetary System." *Wall Street Journal* (23 February).

Bergsten, C. Fred. 1975. *The Dilemmas of the Dollar*. New York: New York University Press.

Bergsten, C. Fred. 1986. "America's Unilateralism." In C. Fred Bergsten, Etienne Davignon, and Isamu Miyazaki, *Conditions for Partnership in International Economic Management*, 3–14. The Triangle Papers no. 32. New York: The Trilateral Commission.

Bergsten, C. Fred. 1988. *America in the World Economy: A Strategy for the 1990s*. Washington: Institute for International Economics.

Bergsten, C. Fred. 1990. "The World Economy After the Cold War." *Foreign Affairs* 69, no. 3 (Summer):96–112.

Bergsten, C. Fred, et al. 1976. *The Reform of International Institutions. The Triangle Papers* no. 11. New York: The Trilateral Commission.

Bryant, R. C. 1987. "Intergovernmental Coordination of Economic Policies: An Interim Stocktaking." In Paul A. Volcker, Ralph C. Bryant, Leonhard Gleske, Gottfried Haberler, Alexandre Lamfalussy, Shijuro Ogata, Jesús Silva-Herzog, Ross M. Starr, James Tobin, and Robert Triffin, *International Monetary Cooperation: Essays in Honor of Henry C. Wallich*. Princeton Essays in International Finance no. 169. Princeton: Princeton University International Finance Section (December).

Buiter, W. H., and J. Eaton. 1985. "Policy Decentralization and Exchange Rate Management in Interdependent Economies." In J. S. Bhandari, ed., *Exchange Rate Management Under Uncertainty*. Cambridge: MIT Press.

Commission of the European Communities. 1990. "One Market, One Money: An Evaluation of Potential Benefits and Costs of Forming an Economic and Monetary Union." *European Economy* 44 (October, whole issue).

Congressional Budget Office. 1988. *The Economic and Budget Outlook: Fiscal Years 1989–1990*. Washington: Congressional Budget Office.

Crockett, Andrew. 1989. "The Role of International Institutions in Surveillance and Policy Coordination." In Ralph C. Bryant, David A. Currie, Jacob A. Frenkel, Paul R. Masson, and Richard Portes, eds., *Macroeconomic Policies in an Interdependent World*, 343–64. Washington: Brookings Institution, Centre for Economic Policy Research, and International Monetary Fund.

Currie, David A., Gerald Holtham, and Andrew Hughes Hallet. 1989. "The Theory and Practice of International Policy Coordination: Does Coordination Pay?" In Ralph C. Bryant, David A. Currie, Jacob A. Frenkel, Paul R. Masson, and Richard Portes, eds., *Macroeconomic Policies in an Interdependent World,* 1–46. Washington: Brookings Institution, Centre for Economic Policy Research, and International Monetary Fund.

Destler, I. M., and C. Randall Henning. 1989. *Dollar Politics: Exchange Rate Policymaking in the United States.* Washington: Institute for International Economics.

Dominguez, Kathryn, and Jeffrey Frankel. 1990. "Does Foreign Exchange Intervention Matter? Disentangling the Portfolio and Expectations Effects for the Mark." Cambridge, MA: John F. Kennedy School of Government, Harvard University; and Berkeley: Department of Economics, University of California, Berkeley (mimeographed, April).

Edison, Hali J. 1990. "Foreign Currency Operations: An Annotated Bibliography." *International Finance Discussion Papers* no. 380. Washington: Board of Governors of the Federal Reserve System (May).

Edison, Hali J., and Michael Melvin. 1990. "The Determinants and Implications of the Choice of an Exchange Rate System." In William S. Haraf and Thomas D. Willett, eds., *Monetary Policy for a Volatile Global Economy,* 1–43. Washington: AEI Press.

Eichengreen, Barry. 1985. "International Policy Coordination in Historical Perspective: A View from the Interwar Years." In Willem H. Buiter and Richard C. Marston, eds., *International Economic Policy Coordination,* 151–52. New York: Cambridge University Press.

Emminger, Otto. 1984. "International Cooperation—A Personal View." In Marjorie Deane and Robert Pringle, eds., *Economic Cooperation from the Inside.* New York: Group of Thirty.

Executive Office of the President and Office of Management and Budget. 1990. *Budget of the United States Government: Fiscal Year 1990,* 3–12. Washington: Government Printing Office.

Feldstein, Martin. 1986. "New Evidence on the Effects of Exchange Rate Intervention." *NBER Working Paper* no. 2052. Cambridge, MA: National Bureau of Economic Research.

Feldstein, Martin. 1988a. "Distinguished Lecture on Economics in Government: Thinking About International Economic Coordination." *Journal of Economic Perspectives 2,* no. 2:3–13.

Feldstein, Martin, ed. 1988b. *International Economic Cooperation.* Chicago: University of Chicago Press.

Feldstein, Martin. 1990. "Time to Bid Farewell to the Louvre Accord." *Financial Times* (London, 29 March).

Fischer, Stanley. 1988. "International Macroeconomic Policy Cooperation." In Martin Feldstein, ed., *International Economic Cooperation.* Chicago: University of Chicago Press.

Frankel, Jeffrey. 1987. "Obstacles to International Economic Policy Coordination." *IMF Working Papers* no. 87/28. Washington: International Monetary Fund.

Frankel, Jeffrey. 1991a. "International Nominal Targeting (INT): A Proposal for

Overcoming Obstacles to Policy Coordination." In John McCallum and Robert Mundell, eds., *Global Disequilibrium*. Montreal: McGill-Queen's University Press (forthcoming).

Frankel, Jeffrey. 1991b. "The Making of Exchange Rate Policy in the 1980s." In Martin Feldstein, ed., *American Economic Policy in the 1980s* (forthcoming).

Frankel, Jeffrey A., and Katharine A. Rockett. 1988. "International Macroeconomic Policy Coordination When Policy-makers Do Not Agree on the Model." *American Economic Review* 78, no. 3:318–40.

Frenkel, Jacob A., and Morris Goldstein, 1986. *A Guide to Target Zones*. IMF Staff Papers no. 33. Washington: International Monetary Fund (December): 633–73.

Frenkel, Jacob A., Morris Goldstein, and Paul R. Masson. 1990. "The Rationale for, and Effects of, International Economic Policy Coordination." In W. Branson, J. Frenkel, and M. Goldstein, eds., *International Policy Coordination and Exchange Rate Fluctuations*, 9–62. Chicago: University of Chicago Press.

Funabashi, Yoichi. 1989. *Managing the Dollar: From the Plaza to the Louvre*, 2nd ed. Washington: Institute for International Economics.

Group of Ten. 1985. "The Functioning of the International Monetary System." Supplement to *IMF Survey*, 14 (July).

Group of Thirty. 1988. *International Macroeconomic Policy Coordination*. New York: Group of Thirty.

Guth, Wilfried, ed. 1988. *Economic Policy Coordination*. Hamburg: HWWA; and Washington: International Monetary Fund.

Gyohten, Toyoo. 1988. "Comment." In Wilfried Guth, ed., *Economic Policy Coordination*, 39. Hamburg: HWWA; and Washington: International Monetary Fund.

Holtham, Gerald. 1989. "German Macroeconomic Policy and the 1978 Bonn Summit." In Richard N. Cooper, Barry Eichengreen, C. Randall Henning, Gerard Holtham, and Robert D. Putnam, *Can Nations Agree? Issues in International Economic Cooperation*, 12–140. Washington: Brookings Institution.

Horne, Jocelyn, and Paul R. Masson. 1988. "Scope and Limits of International Economic Cooperation and Policy Coordination." *IMF Staff Papers*, 35, no. 3 (June):259–96. Washington: International Monetary Fund.

International Monetary Fund. 1988. "Exchange Rate Developments Since the Louvre Accord" (Supplementary Note 2). *World Economic Outlook* (April).

International Monetary Fund. 1989. *World Economic Outlook* (April).

International Monetary Fund. 1990. *World Economic Outlook* (October).

Jurgensen Report. 1983. *Report of the Working Group on Exchange Market Intervention*. Washington: US Treasury (March).

Katzenstein, Peter J. 1978. *Between Power and Plenty: Foreign Economic Policies of Advanced Industrial States*. Madison: University of Wisconsin Press.

Kenen, Peter B. 1986. "International Money and Macroeconomics: An Agenda for Research." Presented at the Second Biennial Conference of Research Institutes, organized by the Institute for International Economics, Washington (September).

Kenen, Peter B. 1990. "The Coordination of Macroeconomic Policies." In W. Branson, J. Frenkel, and M. Goldstein, eds., *International Policy Coordination and Exchange Rate Fluctuations*, 63–108. Chicago: University of Chicago Press.

Loehnis, Anthony. 1989. "The International Monetary System in the 1990s." London: S.G. Warburg (mimeographed, July).

McKibbin, Warwick J., and Jeffrey D. Sachs. 1991. *Macroeconomic Interdependence and Cooperation in the World Economy* (forthcoming).

McKinnon, Ronald I. 1988. "Monetary and Exchange Rate Policies for International Financial Stability: A Proposal." *Journal of Economic Perspectives* 2, no. 1 (Winter): 38.

Marris, Stephen. 1986. *Managing the World Economy: Economics, Institutions and Politics.* Professor Dr. Gaston Eyskens Lectures, Katholieke Universiteit Leuven (mimeographed).

Marris, Stephen. 1987. *Deficits and the Dollar: The World Economy at Risk.* POLICY ANALYSES IN INTERNATIONAL ECONOMICS 14, rev. ed. Washington: Institute for International Economics.

Morgan Guaranty Trust Company. 1987. "Global Growth and Adjustment at Risk." *World Financial Markets* (September-October). New York: Morgan Guaranty Trust Company.

Obstfeld, Maurice. 1990. "The Effectiveness of Foreign-Exchange Intervention: Recent Experience, 1985–1988." In W. Branson, J. Frenkel, and M. Goldstein, eds., *International Policy Coordination and Exchange Rate Fluctuations,* 197–246. Chicago: University of Chicago Press.

Oudiz, Gilles, and Jeffrey Sachs. 1984. "Macroeconomic Policy Coordination among the Industrial Economies." *Brookings Papers on Economic Activity* 1:1–63.

Padoa-Schioppa, Tommaso. 1985. "Policy Cooperation and the EMS Experience." In Willem H. Buiter and Richard C. Marston, eds., *International Economic Policy Coordination,* 331–34. New York: Cambridge University Press.

Polak, Jacques J. 1988. "Economic Policy Objectives and Policymaking in the Major Industrial Countries." In Wilfried Guth, ed., *Economic Policy Coordination,* 1–43. Hamburg: HWWA; and Washington: International Monetary Fund.

Putnam, Robert D., and Nicholas Bayne. 1987. *Hanging Together: Cooperation and Conflict in Seven-Power Summits.* Cambridge, MA: Harvard University Press.

Putnam, Robert D., and C. Randall Henning. 1989. "The Bonn Summit of 1978: A Case Study in Coordination." In Richard N. Cooper, Barry Eichengreen, C. Randall Henning, Gerard Holtham, and Robert D. Putnam, *Can Nations Agree? Issues in International Economic Cooperation,* 12–140. Washington: Brookings Institution.

Solomon, Robert. 1982. *The International Monetary System, 1945–1976: An Insider's View.* New York: Harper and Row.

Taylor, John B. 1985. "International Coordination in the Design of Macroeconomic Policy Rules." *European Economic Review* 28 (June–July):53—81.

Tietmeyer, Hans. 1988. "Comment." In Wilfried Guth, ed., *Economic Policy Coordination,* 135–41. Hamburg: HWWA; and Washington: International Monetary Fund.

US Treasury. 1990. *Joint Report of the US-Japan Working Group on the Structural Impediments Initiative.* Washington: US Treasury (28 June).

Wallich, Henry C. 1984. "Institutional Cooperation in the World Economy." In Jacob Frenkel et al., eds., *The World Economic System: Performance and Prospects,* 85–99. Dover, MA: Auburn House.

Williamson, John. 1985. *The Exchange Rate System.* POLICY ANALYSES IN INTER-
    NATIONAL ECONOMICS 5, rev. ed. Washington: Institute for International Econom-
    ics (June).
Williamson, John, and Marcus H. Miller. 1987. *Targets and Indicators: A Blueprint
    for the International Coordination of Economic Policy.* POLICY ANALYSES IN
    INTERNATIONAL ECONOMICS 22. Washington: Institute for International Economics
    (September).
Working Group on Exchange Market Intervention. 1983. *Report of the Working
    Group on Exchange Market Intervention* (March).
Zysman, John. "The French State in the International Economy." In Peter J. Katzen-
    stein, ed., *Between Power and Plenty: Foreign Economic Policies of Advanced
    Industrial States,* 255–94. Madison: University of Wisconsin Press.

Other Sources Used

Artis, M. J. 1988. "How Accurate is the World Economic Outlook? A Post Mortem on Short-Term Forecasting at the International Monetary Fund." *Staff Studies for the World Economic Outlook*. Washington: International Monetary Fund (July).

Artis, M. J., and S. Ostry. 1986. *International Economic Policy Coordination*. London: Royal Institute of International Affairs.

Bryant, R. C. 1980. *Money and Monetary Policy in Interdependent Nations*. Washington: Brookings Institution.

Bryant, R. C., Dale W. Henderson, Gerard Holtham, Peter Hooper, and Steven A. Symansky, eds. 1988. *Empirical Macroeconomics for Interdependent Economies*. Washington: Brookings Institution.

Bryant, R. C., David A. Currie, Jacob A. Frenkel, Paul R. Masson, and Richard Portes, eds. 1989. *Macroeconomic Policies in an Interdependent World, 9–10*. Washington: Brookings Institution, Centre for Economic Policy Research, and International Monetary Fund.

Committee for the Study of Economic and Monetary Union. 1989. *Report on Economic and Monetary Union in the European Community*. Luxembourg: Office for Official Publications of the European Communities.

Cooper, Richard N. 1985. "Economic Interdependence and Coordination of Economic Policies." In R. W. Jones and P. B. Kenen, eds., *Handbook of International Economics, vol. II, 1194–1234*. Amsterdam: Elsevier Science Publishers.

Kenen, Peter B. 1989. *Exchange Rates and Policy Coordination*. Ann Arbor: University of Michigan Press.

Rogoff, Kenneth. 1985. "Can International Monetary Policy Cooperation be Counterproductive?" *Journal of International Economics* 18:199–217.

Solomon, Robert. 1984. "Forums for Intergovernmental Consultation About Macroeconomic Policies." *Brookings Discussion Papers in International Economics* no. 16. Washington: Brookings Institution.

Truman, Edwin M. 1989. "Approaches to Managing External Equilibria: Where We Are, Where We Might Be Headed, and How We Might Get There." *International Finance Discussion Papers* no. 342. Washington: Board of Governors of the Federal Reserve System (February).

Other Publications from the Institute

POLICY ANALYSES IN INTERNATIONAL ECONOMICS

BOOKS

IMF Conditionality
John Williamson, editor/*1983*
$35.00 (cloth only)   0-88132-006-4   695 pp

Trade Policy in the 1980s
William R. Cline, editor/*1983*
$35.00 (cloth)   0-88132-008-1   810 pp
$20.00 (paper)   0-88132-031-5   810 pp

Subsidies in International Trade
Gary Clyde Hufbauer and Joanna Shelton Erb/*1984*
$35.00 (cloth only)   0-88132-004-8   299 pp

International Debt: Systemic Risk and Policy Response
William R. Cline/*1984*
$30.00 (cloth only)   0-88132-015-3   336 pp

Trade Protection in the United States: 31 Case Studies
Gary Clyde Hufbauer, Diane E. Berliner, and Kimberly Ann Elliott/*1986*
$25.00   0-88132-040-4   371 pp

Toward Renewed Economic Growth in Latin America
Bela Balassa, Gerardo M. Bueno, Pedro-Pablo Kuczynski, and
Mario Henrique Simonsen/*1986*
$15.00   0-88132-045-5   205 pp

American Trade Politics: System Under Stress
I. M. Destler/*1986*
$30.00 (cloth)   0-88132-058-7   380 pp
$18.00 (paper)   0-88132-057-9   380 pp

The Future of World Trade in Textiles and Apparel
William R. Cline/*1987, rev. ed. June 1990*
$20.00   0-88132-110-9   344 pp

Capital Flight and Third World Debt
Donald R. Lessard and John Williamson, editors/*1987*
(Out of stock)   0-88132-053-6   270 pp

The Canada–United States Free Trade Agreement: The Global Impact
Jeffrey J. Schott and Murray G. Smith, editors/*1988*
$13.95   0-88132-073-0   211 pp

Managing the Dollar: From the Plaza to the Louvre
Yoichi Funabashi/*1988, 2nd ed. rev. 1989*
$19.95   0-88132-097-8   307 pp

World Agricultural Trade: Building a Consensus
William M. Miner and Dale E. Hathaway, editors/*1988*
$16.95   0-88132-071-3   226 pp

Japan in the World Economy
Bela Balassa and Marcus Noland/*1988*
$19.95   0-88132-041-2   306 pp

America in the World Economy: A Strategy for the 1990s
C. Fred Bergsten/*1988*
$29.95 (cloth)   0-88132-089-7   235 pp
$13.95 (paper)   0-88132-082-X   235 pp

United States External Adjustment and the World Economy
William R. Cline/*May 1989*
$25.00   0-88132-048-X   392 pp

Free Trade Areas and U.S. Trade Policy
Jeffrey J. Schott, editor/*May 1989*
$19.95   0-88132-094-3   400 pp

Dollar Politics: Exchange Rate Policymaking in the United States
I. M. Destler and C. Randall Henning/*September 1989*
$11.95   0-88132-079-X   192 pp

Foreign Direct Investment in the United States
Edward M. Graham and Paul R. Krugman/*December 1989*
$11.95   0-88132-074-9   161 pp

Latin American Adjustment: How Much Has Happened?
John Williamson, editor/*April 1990*
$34.95   0-88132-125-7   480 pp

**Completing the Uruguay Round: A Results-Oriented
Approach to the GATT Trade Negotiations**
Jeffrey J. Schott, editor/*September 1990*
$19.95   0-88132-130-3   256 pp

Economic Sanctions Reconsidered (in two volumes)
  History and Current Policy (also sold separately, see below)   288 pp
  Supplemental Case Histories   640 pp
Gary Clyde Hufbauer, Jeffrey J. Schott, and Kimberly Ann Elliott/
2nd ed. December 1990
$65.00 (cloth)   0-88132-115-X   928 pp
$45.00 (paper)   0-88132-105-2   928 pp

Economic Sanctions Reconsidered: History and Current Policy
Gary Clyde Hufbauer, Jeffrey J. Schott, and Kimberly Ann Elliott/
2nd ed. December 1990
$25.00 (paper)   0-88132-140-0   288 pp
$36.00 (cloth)   0-88132-136-2   288 pp

Pacific Basin Developing Countries: Prospects for the Future
Marcus Noland/*January 1991*
$29.95 (cloth)   0-88132-141-9   .250 pp
$19.95 (paper)   0-88132-081-1   250 pp

SPECIAL REPORTS

1 **Promoting World Recovery: A Statement on Global
   Economic Strategy**
   by Twenty-six Economists from Fourteen Countries/*December 1982*
   (Out of print)   0-88132-013-7   45 pp

2 **Prospects for Adjustment in Argentina, Brazil, and Mexico:
   Responding to the Debt Crisis**
   John Williamson, editor/*June 1983*
   (Out of print)   0-88132-016-1   71 pp

3 **Inflation and Indexation: Argentina, Brazil, and Israel**
   John Williamson, editor/*March 1985*
   (Out of print)   0-88132-037-4   191 pp

4 **Global Economic Imbalances**
   C. Fred Bergsten, editor/*March 1986*
   $25.00 (cloth)   0-88132-038-2   126 pp
   $10.00 (paper)   0-88132-042-0   126 pp

FORTHCOMING

TO ORDER PUBLICATIONS PLEASE WRITE OR CALL US AT:
Institute for International Economics
Publications Department
11 Dupont Circle, NW
Washington, DC 20036-1207
FAX: 202-328-5432
202-328-9000; 1-800-229-ECON

82923
42

POLICY ANALYSES IN INTERNATIONAL ECONOMICS 30

Economic Policy Coordination: Requiem or Prologue?
Wendy Dobson

The Group of 7 (G-7) process for coordinating economic policy is the latest attempt by the industrialized nations to manage an increasingly integrated world economy. Since its establishment at the 1986 Tokyo summit, however, the accomplishments of the G-7 have been modest and its tasks are largely unfulfilled. The G-7 is regarded in many quarters as irrelevant—at a time when rapid changes in the world economy may demand greater cooperation among the leading economies.

Now is the time to strengthen the G-7 process, not to bury it, concludes Wendy Dobson, formerly Canada's Associate Deputy Minister of Finance and representative to the "G-7 deputies." Dobson assesses how governments have pursued policy coordination since the creation of the G-7 and evaluates their accomplishments. Based on this analysis, she makes five proposals to improve the functioning of the G-7 and thus the future effectiveness of the coordination process.

OTHER PUBLICATIONS FROM THE INSTITUTE FOR INTERNATIONAL ECONOMICS

POLICY ANALYSES IN INTERNATIONAL ECONOMICS Series

ISBN 0-88132-102-8

Institute for International Economics
11 Dupont Circle, NW
Washington, DC 20036-1207
(202) 328-9000 FAX: (202) 328-5432

ISBN 0-88132-102-8

90000>

9 780881 321029